Pratichāyā
Reflection

Mamatha Prabhakar

Credits

Editor and Poet - Raji Rajan

Editor - Samarth Nair

Proofreader – Suma Nagaraj

Sketch Artist - Raghupathi Sringeri

Eye Image sketch – Vaishnavi Ramprasad

Creative consultant - Pannaga Prabhakar

Network consultant – Karthik Prabhakar

Book Title and Cover Design - Sumit Nair and Sidhant Nair

ISBN number: 978-1-7354515-0-3

Author's Note

'Pratichaya', a Sanskrit word for 'Reflection', is a tribute to my father K.G. Prabhakar that captures his life's journey in short stories. Recently, my father told me that he had not achieved much in his life and wished that he could have done more. I smiled at this statement. My father who came in penniless to the city, looked after and nurtured his siblings, and helped hundreds of people along the way was still pondering on what his achievements were. His story to us is no less than a fairy tale. It is truly a rags-to-riches story. A story that should be told to the next generation. The hardships he went through and the sacrifices he had to make are exemplary. The beautiful experiences that my father has shared with us is what I have tried to weave into this book. My father is a half glass-full kind of person. His optimism is very contagious. A self-made man, a proud man, a man who does not show his grievances but always sees the sunny side to every situation in life. His sense of humor in all adversities is also so unique, he makes people around him smile through their struggles. To me, my father has been my teacher, my mentor, my guide, and my inspiration. This book is a humble effort to showcase his amazing journey. My father's full name is Kuderu, the village he came from, Gopalaswamy which is his father's name, and Prabhakar which means the maker of light in Sanskrit, a very ancient language of Hinduism: Kuderu Gopalaswamy Prabhakar. True to his name, he made his own light, and much like the sun, he gave new hope and life to many along the way.

I want to thank Raji, my soul sister who is also a student of my father's, for graciously editing this book. The beautiful poems in this book are written by her. Samarth, my son for final editing of the stories. His challenge was to converge American English, British English, Indian slang, and the regional dialect to a perfect combination in the stories. Pannaga, my sister, who diligently sent the ideas and details for the sketches. Karthik, my brother, for overseeing the progress and getting us all the necessary resources and listening to all the stories while I unfolded them into a book. Sumit, my husband, for encouraging and believing in me. I owe this book to him. I am grateful for his support. And to both my kids Sidhant and Samarth, whose infinite love I am blessed with.

I hope you enjoy the stories and the extraordinary journey of my father K.G. Prabhakar.

Sincere thanks,

Mamatha Prabhakar

Amma - Forever in our hearts

Contents

Lush and green
In fullness of joy.
Stands at dawn
The tree, its life.
Letting the sun through
Shining from within.
Soaked in warmth
Of love and hope.
Promises until eternity
Dreams until dusk.
A song of the breeze
And a dance with ease
A twirl and twist
The tree, its life.

Childhood

Rangamma Akka

It was in the year 1945, two years before India's independence, that Prabhakar was born to Kamalamma and Gopalaswamy in a quiet, small house in Mysore.

Gopalaswamy worked as a station master in the Railways. He had set up his home with his wife, Kamalamma in Hubli. When Prabhakar was two years old, he was left with his grandma Rangamma and his maternal uncles in Mysuru, which was back then called Mysore. Mysore was the capital of the Kingdom of Mysore and bore a touch of royalty in every sense. His maternal uncles at the time did not have any kids of their own and perhaps it was thought that Prabhakar would get maximum attention from everyone. He had five siblings in quick succession as was the case in most families of the time. Kamalamma was unable to give much attention to Prabhakar, who by then was considered 'grown-up' as compared to his younger siblings. The attention he got from his grandmother was more than he got from his parents.

Amidst the royalty of Mysore was simplicity and contentment of people belonging to any class. Born into and being brought up in a lower middle-class family, Prabhakar too was a happy and contented child. *Akka*, as Prabhakar called Rangamma, was his primary caretaker and guardian, with whom he spent most of his time. Rangamma, a widow with a shaved head, was a loud and protective matriarch, who in every sense was Prabhakar's guardian. She never missed a chance to combatively shoo away neighbors if they came to her doorstep with complaints about her dear grandson's mischief. Bearing a stern look and a straight gait, with hands on her hips or waving in denial, she would declare, "Do not blame my little boy, I do not believe a word you say about him. Surely, he is not the one to initiate mischief!" She would be firm about her statement in Prabhakar's defense. Little did she care what people thought of her aggressive and argumentative tone.

Prabhakar was homeschooled by his grandmother and uncles in his early years. When he aged up to seven years of age, it was decided that he would be admitted to 'Government Primary school' in Chamundipuram for 3rd grade. His maternal uncle approached the school justifiably for admission to the 3rd grade. The headmaster looked up through the top of the frame of his thick-rimmed glasses and shook his head in disagreement. "As is the rule," he cleared his throat and said "if a child has never been to school, 1st grade is where he needs to begin. How can I skip two grades and admit him to 3rd grade? He would know nothing of what was taught in the previous two grades!", bringing his hand down to the table with seasoned authority. Prabhakar's uncle did not know what to say in response. He returned home with Prabhakar in disappointment and narrated the incident to Rangamma. Oh, but she would have none of it! She was very angry and decided to take the matter into her own hands. She went back to school with Prabhakar. Prabhakar silently went along, sensing well that his *Akka* was in one of her determined moods in his favor. Rangamma breezed into the Headmaster's office with presumed permission and demanded Prabhakar's admission to the 3rd grade. She had prepared enough in support of her argument. She pulled Prabhakar forward and asked him to recite poems and mathematical tables he had learned at home in the past two years. Prabhakar was smart enough to deliver them with ease and confidence. After all, *Akka* had made sure he learned them all well! Prabhakar went on with the recitation as Rangamma *Akka* looked at him lovingly and the headmaster held his head in his hand. This boy was not going to stop anytime soon! The headmaster sheepishly gave in and asked Prabhakar to select any class he wished to sit in. Thus, began Prabhakar's long and fruitful education journey.

Such was Rangamma's power of persuasion. Prabhakar recalls with fond gratitude that it was probably the first and last time any elder person from his family had represented him in his educational career.

One day, Prabhakar and his friends decided to skip school to spend the time playing. Unfortunately, Prabhakar's maternal uncle caught him and his friends playing and diligently carried the news to Rangamma, holding out his hand in accusation with a pointed finger. "You are spoiling him! Look, what he has been up to!" he complained. Rangamma, however, showed no remorse or anger toward Prabhakar's act. Instead, in a calm and monotonous tone, laced with undisguised possessiveness, her words of support for him strung together as easily as ever. "My grandson is not going wayward. He is going to make us all proud one day. Just wait and see". Later that evening, she waited for Prabhakar to return home and gave him an earful for what he had done. That was the bond Rangamma and Prabhakar shared. She guarded him very closely and only she could reprimand her child. So deep and intense was this maternal affection, that Prabhakar almost stopped waiting for the periodic visits from his parents and siblings. Strangely, he yearned to return to his *Akka* if he was sent to Hubli to spend a few days of break as well. Prabhakar cherished this bond and the privileged attention and protection he received from *Akka*, for years to come.

There were times when Prabhakar too was embarrassed by Rangamma, because his friends mocked him about the lady with a shaved head who often spoke in a loud voice. In pre-Independence India of the 1930s, conservative Hindu traditions were more prevalent. Widowed women had to leave behind their colorful saris, part with their jewelry, and shave their heads. Rangamma *Akka* had followed all these traditions diligently. Prabhakar had hated the traditions even as a child. Caste system and ritualism were deep rooted in the lives of the common man back then and the plight of widows was very disturbing. He had witnessed a few widows from his family who ate from food served on the floor as part of the ritual. Prabhakar had often thought, "This is so unhygienic and inhuman!" He grew up averse to these traditions and little did he realize then, that in his journey of life, he would be defying some of those traditional norms for his family.

He always fondly remembered *Akka* as the superhero grandmother who he wished would have lived long enough to proudly watch him grow into a handsome, successful, and progressive young man.

Anna

Anna, as Prabhakar called his father Gopalaswamy, was a pleasing personality: tall and smart with curly hair. He was a very simple, intelligent, and kindhearted person who was always ready to help his kith and kin. Much loved by everyone around him, he was a man of few words. His father had remarried after his mother's untimely death, and he along with his two younger brothers grew up quite neglected by his parents. With circumstances being not so pleasant, Anna had to take up a job to earn and look after his two siblings.

When Prabhakar was a child, Gopalaswamy would visit him in Mysore once every six months. Indian Railways was going through a major change after Independence and the zonal system was being put in place. Southern Railways was the first zone to be formed and with all the reorganization taking place, it was understaffed. Postings were in accordance with need and demand and leave of absence was not easily accepted. Gopalaswamy, like many of his co-workers, could only visit his family and hometown rarely.

As a child, Prabhakar would eagerly wait for *Anna's* visit to Mysore. Anna had a good number of friends in Mysore who would also await his visits and their meet at a popular hangout, GTR café. Famous for its crispy hot *dosas*[1] and aromatic, freshly brewed filter coffee, GTR was one of the few popular eat-out joints of those times. Dining out was rare and considered a luxury. So, it was with great pride that *Anna* would take his friends out and treat them, though on a meagre salary. The friends spent a good long time together through laughter and stories, sipping coffee from steel tumblers and spicing up their *dosas* with light gossip. Prabhakar often wished they would not stay long with Anna because he would hardly get time with him, the visits being far apart and for just a few days each time. "Why can't Rangamma *Akka* chase Anna's friends away, like she does to mine?", he wondered in resentment.

Anna's attention was precious to Prabhakar. Occasionally, *Anna* would look down and lovingly smile at him and ruffle his hair. This filled Prabhakar's heart with immense joy. He would admiringly gaze at Anna, holding onto bars of half-open windows and soak in his presence as much as he could with the fewest blinks that he could manage, because he knew that Anna would be gone soon and it would be yet another long wait before his next visit.

Anna was a chain smoker. Prabhakar would often see him light his cigarettes in style and watch him with great admiration from a distance. Anna would hold the cigarette with such confidence, of a popular brand called Berkley, and with

---

[1] *Dosas – Rice Crepes*

inimitable style, he took each puff with a deep long breath and exhaled the smoke with his head held high. "Oh *Anna*! Why won't you stay longer here?" Prabhakar wished, sad but hoping that it would happen someday.

It was sports day at school and Prabhakar, in 3rd grade then, was very excited. His father had just arrived from Hubli that morning and Prabhakar was determined to get the first prize in running and make his father proud of him. Prabhakar had been practicing hard on the muddy track for days. After all, he had to win, and Anna had to know that he was doing his best in school. Yes, he had to win!

On the big day, the school sports ground was all cleared and set to hold the events: tracks drawn out in long parallel lines with white chalk powder, the start and finish lines clearly marked with two poles on either end. The finishing line had 'winning' flags tied to it and Prabhakar's eye was all set on it.

The game began and during the semi-final run, Prabhakar's foot slipped off the track and he fell on his knee. His knee got scraped, and his eyes welled up, more in pain and a little from the mud that had risen to the air with his fall. But the pain of the injury was not more than the pain in his heart. He was shattered. What had he done? In his eagerness to win, he had hastily jeopardized his chances by falling. But he would not fall in the eyes of his Anna, he was determined. He fought all the pain and when the whistle blew for the final round, his mind was all set. His pain bothered him but all he could see was the proud look his father would have on his face, when he showed him the prize. He ran with all his strength and will. He came in second and won a rubber snake as a prize.

Slightly limping with his bruised knee, he ran to Anna to show off his prize. How happy he will be, he thought. He will embrace me in a hug and pat my back with utmost pride, Prabhakar thought and smiled. He saw Anna sleeping on the cot as he sneaked in eagerly and dropped the rubber snake on him

Anna woke up with a start and jumped off the cot in fear. Assuming that this was Prabhakar's prank, he slapped him hard across his face, which had already turned pale in fear. He scolded him and signaled him away with a sway of his hand. Prabhakar's eyes welled with tears and now, he let them flow. All he had wanted was for Anna to be happy. He ran away as fast as he could, the pain in his knee strangely no longer as bad.

Late into the night, when Prabhakar did not return home, Rangamma went looking for him and found him sitting under the tree, sulking, with tear stains on his flushed cheeks. Prabhakar looked up and instantly felt a sigh of relief when he saw *Akka*. He had been waiting all evening, to be found and taken home, instead of returning on his own. That day, he was bruised in more ways than one.

Shripathi

Prabhakar was very fond of his maternal uncle, Shripathi *mava*[2]. Shripathi *mava* was actively involved in theater and would perform *Harikathe*, an ancient tradition of storytelling which essentially is a one-person performance of folklore songs, stories, and drama, based on mythology. His performances would be in the local village tent or in an open space in the village center. *Harikathe* was the main mass entertainment then and was equally enjoyed by people of all ages, sitting around the performer, and listening to stories intently. The

---

[2] *mava – Maternal uncle in Kannada*

performer too would be as involved and be transformed into the character he played at the time.

Shripathi's loud and commanding voice, alongside his facial expressions to emote and enact the scene impressively, brought the strong mythological characters he portrayed to life. His impactful narration and witty comments accompanying his act were always a delight to watch. Prabhakar enjoyed every moment of his *mava's Harikathe* with excitement and admiration, applauding him joyously, with a wide smile. Prabhakar inherited the lighter side of his personality from Shripathi. *Mava* would tell him stories of freedom fights: the struggle, the victory, the sacrifices, all of it. Prabhakar was born two years before India's Independence and the ambience lingered fresh in his imagination. The stories he heard were almost as vivid as they had happened.

A decade after Independence, Shripathi received a letter from the Government of India announcing that he was eligible for a government pension in the capacity of a freedom fighter. Shripathi was ecstatic and unabashedly proud of himself. After all, he had a role to play in getting freedom for his country! "It was not easy", he would say, in his accustomed narrational tone. "Do you know how much torture I had to face while fighting the British?" With meaningful pauses to intensify his narrative, he would go on to tell Prabhakar how he bore the atrocities of the British, all for the love of his motherland.

There was however a twist in his tale, which most of the village folks knew. Some of them who were witness to Shripathi's "freedom fight" had spread the word about how the story actually transpired. They said he was lucky to be in the right place at the right time. It was a day of protests, against the British, when Shripathi was present somewhere close to the venue of the protest, watching the rehearsal of a play. The police had to control the protesters and whisked away a few to exercise control on the situation. One among them was Shripathi too, as he was in the vicinity. He spent the next couple of days in jail and finally when he was released, people hailed him as a freedom fighter!

Prabhakar knew this truth, but he never asked his Shripathi *mava* about it. Instead, he enjoyed listening to the repeated narration of stories of struggle when *mava* had stood bravely against the British. Prabhakar would cheer his bravery with undeterred admiration each time.

Years later, Prabhakar witnessed an incident in the factory where Shripathi *mava* worked. There was a workers' union strike where the factory workers were demanding better working conditions. Police arrived to see that the situation was under control and no untoward incident occurred. Prabhakar was in the factory at the time and saw Shripathi running without any hesitation towards the police van and seating himself inside the van. He wanted to make sure he was safe and get away from the crowd.

"Such was his bravery!" Prabhakar thought and chuckled in amusement.

For all the theatrics his uncle did in real life and for all his performances on stage, Shripathi, as always, remained Prabhakar's adorable *mava*.

Dhagli

Prabhakar was the oldest of six children and this gave him both the authority over his younger siblings as well as the responsibility to care for them. Prabhakar was always assigned chores that started early in the morning. The first being washing of all the younger ones, after they finished their morning jobs.

Every day, he had to wake up on time to sit outside their toilets until the job was done and the 'call' came. At times, his eyes would shut for a few seconds, but he would jolt himself out of his sleep and intermittently repeat *"Ayitheno?"* ("Are you done?")

Among all his siblings, Prabhakar's youngest sister, Viji, short for Vijaya Lakshmi was the most adorable. She was several years younger to Prabhakar. She loved Prabhakar with all her little heart and followed him lovingly everywhere. Prabhakar too could not stop her from being around him almost always. After all, this little sister, was his ardent admirer!

Prabhakar had named Viji, 'Dhagli', a short form for *Dhagalbaazi*, a fighter! She too would respond promptly to her 'Anna' when he called her Dhagli. She was always cheerful, bubbly and loved to talk. She would hop and skip behind Prabhakar, be excited with little things and draw Prabhakar's attention to share her joy. "Anna, look at this!", or "Anna, did you see that?!' Prabhakar would listen to her non-stop chatter and she always followed him like a little puppy, one with no tail.

One day, Prabhakar came back from school to be told that Viji had taken ill and was running a high fever. The doctors could not diagnose the cause of the fever and the prescribed medication was not helping her. She suffered for days and the household was worried and quiet. The doctors suspected that prolonged malnutrition must have made her sick. It was not uncommon in those times to have children suffer from malnutrition and bear dire consequences of it - sometimes even leading to death. Too many mouths to feed resulting in insufficient food intake for all, was a major reason. Lack of adequate knowledge of proper diet and care for young mothers and children was another considerable factor. The economic conditions were not supportive either.

Prabhakar wished he had the money to get her the best treatment. All he could do now was pray for her recovery. He prayed hard every day. He missed Dhagli's playful self and all her antics around him. He prayed so much for his Dhagli, but his prayers went unanswered. Viji, his brave fighter, lost the battle. She succumbed to the deadly disease and Prabhakar lost his dear little admirer forever.

Throughout his life, he had many people who appreciated and commended him for his achievements, but none brought him as much happiness as the innocent, undying and loving admiration Dhagli had for him. Dhagli was and will remain his first and greatest fan, fighter, and follower.

Raju

Prabhakar studied in a local school in Mysore, called Sharda Vilas High School. The school was started way back in 1861 as an Anglo-Sanskrit school, as directed by the-then ruler of Mysore state, Mummadi Sri Krishnaraja Wodeyar. His Royal Highness had a vision of making Mysore a center for formal primary and secondary education. The school was initially housed in a temple but was later shifted to Lansdowne building. The school playground, though small, was perfect for pre-lunch games and the boys would play kho-kho[3] which is a tag game, *kabaddi*[4], another popular tag and tackle game, and cricket.

Prabhakar made many friends in school, but the closest of them all were Murthy and Chandru, both brilliant boys, with whom Prabhakar spent a lot of his study time.

Joint families lived in ancestral homes back then. Family members of three to four generations living together was a common tradition. Prabhakar too lived in a house with a family of almost fifteen members. The house buzzed with activities most of the day, not allowing for quiet time that Prabhakar needed to do his studies. He found himself studying under streetlights often. Sometimes, when the weather was not favorable, he would go to the local *dhobi*[5] who served the residents of the neighborhood with laundry service in a small, well-lit, sheltered place - his own laundromat.

Raju, the *dhobi*, was a jovial young immigrant from Andhra Pradesh who worked hard day and night, seemingly without tiring himself out from the mundane task of ironing clothes. He would merrily sing through the night, gently swaying his head in rhythm, his heavy coal iron box moving in perfect rows in unison. Humming and singing '*Yedu Kondala Vada, Ekkadunnavayya*', a famous Telugu devotional song, he meticulously ironed and folded clothes, piling them up neatly in a corner, to be delivered back to houses the next day. His deep voice wafted through the thin air into the night. Prabhakar would find a bright study corner and settle down to deeply focus and solve his math and physics problems. Years later,

---

[3] *kho-kho – popular contact team sport played in India*
[4] *kabaddi - popular contact team sport played in India*
[5] *dhobi - a caste group of India whose traditional occupation is washing clothes.*

this favorite laundromat that provided him a place to study was sold and Raju was untraceable. Folks in the neighborhood said that he had returned to his hometown in Andhra Pradesh. Deep down in his heart, Prabhakar knew his wish to see Raju again would only remain a wish.

Raju and his kind and giving spirit remained an inspiration in Prabhakar's life for years to come. Though Raju had very little space where he had heaps of clothes piled all the time, he had a large heart to make that little sheltered space for Prabhakar to study: a small haven protecting him from bad weather, unruly drunkards, and hungry, barking street dogs.

Prabhakar had just one thought in return for Raju's kind deed. He would always keep his doors open for children who needed a place to study. No space is smaller or bigger than what the heart can contain, he learned, as one of life's earliest lessons.

The Anonymous Cricket Club

In the era where Prabhakar was growing up, cricket was a favorite pastime sport for children and young adults. There were different forms of cricket that were seen played by kids. 'Road cricket' was one. 'Ground cricket' another. 'Cork ball cricket' one, 'rubber ball cricket' another. The game, brought into India by the British, was the one thing they left behind that was much loved by most people. The equipment used for the game also varied and was innovative and impressive. Sticks or blocks of stone for stumps and even wooden rulers or old pencil boxes were used for bails.

Prabhakar and his friends were cricket lovers too. There was a playground called Boothala Pitch Playground near where they lived. A little space in the playground was enough for them to have a good game going. The playground had a huge tree with a stone bench and in the shade of its wide branches, there was respite for folks to rest, catch up on gossip or share news on an upcoming event. The floating population in this hub were the spectators of their game.

One hot afternoon when they were playing, they were approached by a group of boys who wanted a challenge game of cricket with them. Challenge game meant a group of boys would form a team and would challenge another group of boys for a match to be played. Captains for each team would be nominated and the number of players and balls to be bowled would be decided. *"Challenge matchge barthira?"* a tall lanky kid asked Prabhakar. Seeing Murthy nod, Prabhakar agreed to the challenge match. They were a formidable team of four and with great pride decided to call themselves 'The Anonymous Cricket Club'. While Murthy was the captain of the team, Prabhakar was the main bowler. Prabhakar bowled with great ease and effortlessly rolled out spins with a swift twist of his hand. Since the other team had all the 11 players required for a team, it was discussed that they would share the fielders for both sides. The game was set for the following Sunday. And so, the captain of the team, Murthy, now a celebrated leader and founder of a billion-dollar company, would lead the cricket team to win against all odds. The match was played against a full-fledged 11-players' team! That was a proud moment for the boys indeed.

These little joys of childhood when his clothes and hands were dirty playing in the dust, his hair was messy, were some of the most delightful moments that would be etched in Prabhakar's memory for years to come.

Fun at School

The boys at school were playful and naughty, just as any generation can be at that age. School time was perfect for them to unleash their witty and mischievous selves.

Teachers of those times bore a typical look in their attire. They wore 'a *panche or a dhoti*[6], paired with an *angi*[7]or shirt and coat.

Slightly overgrown hair accessorized with a *Gandhi topi*[8] or *peta*[9]. Rows of wooden benches, some shaky with age and others weighed down by knowledge adorned the classroom. The classroom was small, yet large enough to accommodate study and fun. The grilled windows were not only the breaks in the otherwise monotonous, white-washed walls, but they were also a source of relief from mundane lessons so the children could glance at the seemingly more interesting world outside class.

There were times the students were given lessons to be read through in class when the teacher would fall into a slumber with his head swinging down or sideways in a state of unapologetic sleep! Opportunities to show their 'skills' were much awaited by the naughty boys in the class during this time. The most daring boy would slyly approach the teacher who would be enjoying his power nap. Muffling giggles with a palm and holding his breath to make sure nothing interrupted the master plan, the 'brave' boy would tactfully tie the teacher's hair into a nice round lemon! The whole class would remain silent in dedicated teamwork, except for a few escaped giggles. Once the task was complete, the suppressed giggles would break into laughter. The heroic act was much admired and the boy who did it would be applauded with admiring glances and nods and meaningful hand signs.

Prabhakar also recalls how all his friends would smartly scatter and rush to find their seats in the last rows for the Math class wisely, to avoid being sprayed by the teacher who would accidentally spit when speaking!

---

[6] *Panche or a dhoti – a type of sarong, which is the ethnic costume for men*
[7] *Angi – shirt in Kannada*
[8] *Gandhi topi – a white colored side cap made from Khadi takes its name after Indian leader Mahatma Gandhi.*
[9] *Peta – a turban in Kannada.*

While these instances were fun and memorable, Prabhakar often remembered his teachers with great reverence. Their high morals and integrity were commendable and stayed with the students as lessons for life. One such moral he recollects is the one he imbibed from his chemistry teacher, K.V. Narayan, who warned children during their laboratory sessions to not waste more salt than needed for their experiments. They were strictly instructed to take only as much as required. Salt, which was then the cheapest and most common ingredient though, was also to be preserved and not misused because it was part of school property. In a way, this taught the students a feeling of responsibility and accountability towards public property and the community at large. Prabhakar too believes that this sense of responsibility and lessons he learned from his eminent teachers were the ones he handed down to his students later in his life, when he himself became an educator by profession.

Geography as a subject was always considered dry and uninteresting, with just imaginary lines and countries to study about. However, for Prabhakar, the memory of geography classes was different. His teacher, Sosale Rajagopal Iyengar, made the subject interesting with engaging discussions and impressive study materials. He explained the geography of the world in class with a globe created from a coconut shell on which the North Pole, South Pole, longitudes, and latitudes were all drawn with as much accuracy as possible. He and his students travelled the world together using their imagination with a coconut shell! In the years that followed, Prabhakar learned that for a teacher to be good in his profession and for students to learn well, the inspiration comes from simple things. During one such interactive class, when the teacher was holding his globe high and pointing his stick to the geographical boundaries explaining a lesson, Murthy was caught bending over excitedly to share a quick chat with another boy across the bench. The teacher went over to Murthy and tapped his head with the coconut, to draw his attention back to the discussion. To this day, Prabhakar believes that Murthy was blessed by that coconut. Why not, it must be so! To put it in a 'nutshell', Murthy went on to be a very successful entrepreneur.

Vasappa

The charm of Mysore was attributed to its beautiful, structured villages which were simple yet self-sufficient, and complemented the royalty of the city remarkably well. The villages, rich in resources and in goodness of its people, left a mark of beauty and tradition, which to this day is palpable in the city famed for its architecture.

Malavalli was one such village where Prabhakar's aunt, Kittama, lived. He would spend his summer holidays with his aunt, enjoying the peace and simple joys of the place that even mundane routine offered. The sound of morning chores seemed synchronized in every home. Turbaned men heading out before dawn, with bullocks pulling carts and ploughs to the fields, the bells around their necks jingling, women drawing water from the wells to fill their clay pots, and getting their kitchen firewood warmed up were common scenes in the early hours of the day. The morning bird song and the aroma of fresh leaves and budding fruit trees added to the welcoming of a new day. His aunt's father-in-law Vasappa, an eighty-five-year-old man, lived in the same house. He was very fond of Prabhakar and was happy to have him for company during summer. Vasappa was visually impaired with cataracted eyes, but in those days, surgery was a big deal and Vasappa had learned to live with his limited sight. He was a fiercely independent man. Even at that age, he would walk two kilometers every morning from the house to his fields.

A variety of trees lined Vasappa's fields: mainly tamarind, mango, and coconut trees. The branches that spread out from the mango trees served as perfect cool shade to beat the scorching heat of summer. The leaves of coconut trees swayed slightly in the warm breeze and stood tall with the morning rays glistening on them. Vasappa would find his way to a small pond in the middle of the fields and bathe in the water that was naturally warm, followed by his meditation and prayers.

Prabhakar would accompany Vasappa every morning on this daily routine and he often marveled at how Vasappa would find his way to the pond without any help. Prabhakar recollects an incident on one such walk back from the fields. As they headed home, they heard hushed voices and rustling of leaves coming from the fields. Vasappa immediately stood still and turned his head in the direction of the sound, twitching his eyebrows to intently listen. Prabhakar too turned around, to find that there were a few people stealing tamarind from the trees! Even before Prabhakar could take the credit for reporting the incident to Vasappa, he was in for a surprise. Vasappa had identified the crime with his sharp senses and shouted out in a warning tone. He raised his cane with a swish and aimed it towards the direction of the noise, hurling it up into the air. As Prabhakar gaped in utter astonishment, the cane magically flew with all its might, just like a Javelin throw that Prabhakar had seen during sports events in school. The only difference was that this javelin had a target: the tamarind thieves! It went straight to its target on the tree and hit the thief leaving him in both shock and pain. As soon as the cane hit him, the thief jumped down the tree and scuttled away. The others who watched the trailer of the show too ran away before they could be bestowed with similar punishment from the cane.

Later that day, the village council gathered outside Vasappa's house. The man who was hurt by the cane had brought together a good number of folks from the village to question him. He had raised a complaint that he was nearly maimed by this crazy old man!

Vasappa did not give in. He stood his ground and declared with a thundering voice that he would not allow thieves to loot his fields at the cost of anything. He was visually impaired, but his other senses were as strong as anyone, or maybe stronger. His values too reflected his strong beliefs. He declared with his head raised, "If they wanted tamarind from my field, they should have asked. I would have gladly allowed them to pick some. But theft? No! That is not right!" As the villagers continued to argue, Prabhakar looked on. Here was a man who was so courageous and did not let his shortcoming discourage him from doing right and standing by it, all alone. The eight-year-old and the eighty-five-year-old were two, standing in front of an angry group of people, at least fifty in number! Eventually, the villagers dispersed, mumbling under their breath, and convinced that they had no say to win this argument in their favor. Prabhakar looked up at Vasappa and smiled as he found himself holding his hand. This incident inspired Prabhakar a lot. He had learned a valuable lesson: never to give in to wrongdoings and to face challenges against all odds, come what may.

Shyamanna

Shyamanna was the son of Vasappa. He worked as a constable in the police department and was posted in Mysore. Mysore, the city located near the foothills of the Chamundi Hills is famous for its heritage structures and palaces. In the heart of the city is the opulent Royal Palace, seat of the former ruling Wodeyar dynasty. The city is well known for the festivities that take place during the period of *Dasara*, the state festival of Karnataka. The *Dasara* festivities, which are celebrated over a ten-day period, were first introduced by King Raja Wodeyar I in 1610. The Wodeyars were patrons of art and culture and the ten-day Hindu festival that falls during the month of September or October is celebrated on a grand scale.

Every year, Shyamanna would be assigned to the security personnel team at the Mysore Dasara celebrations. The elaborate festivities include music and dance events and is witnessed by the royal assembly in the special *Darbar*[10] where the living generations of the royal Wodeyar family, special invitees and general public attend the event. The ninth day of the festival marks the worship of the Royal Sword which is taken on a procession with decorated elephants, camels, and horses. The Mysore Palace is brightly lit up with 100,000 lights representing *Lakshadeepa*[11] and on *Vijayadashami*[12], the traditional Dasara procession is taken on the streets of Mysore. The main attraction of the procession on the tenth and concluding day is the idol of Goddess Chamundeshwari seated on a decorated elephant and accompanied by dancers in colorful costumes and loud music bands. In total grandeur, the procession leads the elephant to bring the idol to Banni Mantap, a scared abode under the Banyan Tree. Legend has it that the kings worshipped this tree before heading out to any warfare.

Prabhakar, his friends and siblings loved to be amid the Dasara celebrations. The main excitement for Prabhakar in the whole event was to find Shyamanna in the sizeable crowd and be rewarded for it. None of the festivities with the royal family could beat his excitement to get this mission accomplished. Shyamanna would give him a *paisa*[13] as reward for finding him

---

[10] *Darbar – (in colonial India) a reception, commemorating an occasion.*

[11] *Lakshadeepa – Literal translation for one hundred thousand lamps*

[12] *Vijayadashami12 – popular festival among Hindus signifying good winning over evil.*

[13] *Paisa - Former denomination of the Indian Rupee. Equals 1/100 of the Indian Rupee.*

and Prabhakar would gleefully spend the *paisa* to either buy peanuts or fried *papads* [14]at the festival fair. Finding Shyamanna among thousands of people was not an easy task and it would sometimes take him hours to tower over people's heads and fulfill his mission. The reward was motivating enough for him to put in all his effort. The shining paisa and the tasty treat it could buy him was on his mind while his head turned unfixed in all directions and eyes were wide open, barely blinking in the lookout for Shyamanna.

Prabhakar would sometimes run into Narasimha *mava*, a far relative who was also a constable in Mysore Police. Narasimha *mava* would not give Prabhakar any money. Instead, he would hassle the vendors selling peanuts or corn and command them to give it for free. Prabhakar did not like this; he did not like the fact that these vendors had to give things out of fear of the police. So, he avoided meeting Narsimha *mava*. He would look only for Shyamanna.

Around lunch time every day, the 200-odd officials posted for duty in the celebrations were to be served food traditionally on banana leaves, in a cordoned hall inside the palace. One such festive day, Prabhakar had been looking for Shyamanna all morning and found him only around lunchtime as he was heading towards the hall for lunch. He called out loudly and Shyamanna signaled Prabhakar to follow him into the hall. Mats were drawn out in rows on the floor for people to sit down and eat.

As a known rule, anyone who entered the hall had to leave their footwear outside. Prabhakar too removed his slippers before he entered the hall and waited patiently in a corner for his reward. In a while, a senior police inspector walked in with

---

[14] *Papads – Thin, crisp flatbread*

his boots. There was hustle inside as people looked in both shock and disgust as one of them went up to him to request him to remove his footwear. This irked the police inspector. He did not heed and continued walking in a more authoritative gait. He was the highest-ranking official in the department, and no one had the courage to stop him. They just stared in disbelief and whispered amongst themselves, "He is probably from the northern part of India and does not understand the culture of our state." Shyamanna, however, could not take this insult to his tradition and culture. He steeled himself, walked up to the inspector and requested him in a very humble but firm tone to remove his boots. He went on to explain the reason for their request. The tradition apart, it is not hygienic to walk with dusty footwear into a place where food is served, especially on the floor.

This was it. The inspector had heard too much by now and his ego was bruised. How dare a senior official of his cadre be told what was right! In a fit of anger, he pushed Shyamanna to make his way through and harshly told him to mind his own business. Shyamanna fell back, nearly falling to the floor but got himself upright soon enough and retorted by giving a tight slap to the inspector. Everyone gasped in unison and then there was complete silence in the hall. They all knew the enormity of Shyamanna's act and could only imagine how he would have to face the wrath of the inspector. He may even lose his job! As expected, Shyamanna was suspended with immediate orders from the inspector. There was an inquiry in the higher office of the IG (Inspector General).

Prabhakar had witnessed all this drama. He had feared for Shyamanna. The day of the inquiry arrived. Shyamanna presented himself in the IG's office and was questioned about his act. Without any hesitation, Shyamanna held his head high and said "It was a sacred place Sir, Goddess Annapoorneshwari was present there. It was a sanctorum where *Anna Dhana*[15] which is the rice and meal donation was happening! How could I be a mute witness to disrespect shown in such a place, that too after repeated pleas? I had no choice but to take this step, especially after the inspector physically roughed me up." The Inspector General listened thoughtfully to the narration of the incident and finally with a sigh, looked up at Shyamanna and said, "You have withheld the integrity of the work we do as police. We are here to serve the public and if we do not understand and respect the culture of people regardless of where we come from, we are not fit to be police officers, guarding our country and its people. However, the action you have taken is incomplete and hence, regrettable. You gave him just one slap? Why did you not give him another one on his other cheek?!" Everyone who was present in the hall at that moment and were anxiously awaiting the IG's command on further action, loosened up and smiled. Shyamanna was surprised, relieved, and sensed a feeling of pride, all at once. He was reinstated with honors.

Following this incident, Prabhakar's affection and respect for Shyamanna grew multifold. He was proud of Shyamanna's ideals and it had a significant influence on his life. Prabhakar learned to stand up to authority and to be assertive if something was not right. To never allow a wrongdoing, whether to himself or to anyone or anything around him, became a moral he followed in the later chapters of his life.

---

[15] *Anna Dhana – made up of two words. Anna meaning rice and Dhana meaning donating.*

Rajesh

As a child, Prabhakar hated his name. "Why did Anna give me such an old name? There are so many modern and stylish names like Ramesh, Rajesh and so on. Why the name Prabhakar, oh why? Why did they not think well before naming me?!" he often wondered, helplessly. No, not helplessly for long, though. Prabhakar was not the one to give up easily. He would find himself a nice name and people would thereafter call him by the new name, he declared to himself. As simple as that. He suddenly felt triumphant with his brilliant idea. He gave a good thought and finally decided to name himself 'Rajesh'. Yes,

Rajesh would suit him the most, he decided, and felt a sense of inexplicable pride. He pretended to be Rajesh and began asking people to call him by his brand-new name. He even had a photograph of himself on which he etched his name, 'Rajesh' and went on to learn how to sign by that name. The only person who briefly indulged him in his fad was his maternal uncle's daughter. She preserved his treasured photograph and gave it to his wife years later.

Prabhakar was a lanky kid and he never liked his physicality. He was fascinated by wrestlers and the strong body they had. After a few consultations with friends on food and diet, he decided to make a concoction. He took a large clay pot and put a dozen bananas in it and mixed honey and ghee with it. He hid the pot in the attic so none of his siblings or his cousins, Vishwa and Sheshadri, could reach it. He now dreamed of having the physicality of a bodybuilder. The first day, he had a spoon of the concoction and it was very tasty but as the week passed, it got sour and he could see the froth coming out of this mixture. As the smell got disgusting, he had no choice but to dump it. As he was throwing out the contents, his barber who was passing along asked what he was up to. Prabhakar explained to him "Well, you see, I made this dish with honey, bananas and ghee and I think it has all gone bad". Even as Prabhakar was completing his sentence the barber snatched the pot from Prabhakar and gulped it down. Wiping his mouth, he grinned, "Why waste such rich ingredients? Over the next few months, Prabhakar kept checking on his barber and he was sure the barber had grown a little larger. Prabhakar sighed and thought to himself, "If only I had tolerated the smell and taste".

Prabhakar, like any adolescent going through the transitional stage of physical and psychological development, had hated his name and physicality. Over the years, however, the name 'Rajesh' on the photograph, had been attempted to be slyly overwritten by the name Prabhakar. Perhaps, no one remembered to call him by that name long enough. Perhaps his fascination for a modern name had fizzled out too soon. Perhaps, over time, he decided to accept his originality and his looks and make a name out of Prabhakar and one fine day of awakening, the overwriting had happened. Whatever the reason, Rajesh took a back seat in Prabhakar's life but somehow remained a part of him forever.

Movie Time

Cinema was a good source of entertainment for the boys of those times. Mysore had three theatres: Olympia, Prabha and Ranjith. Movies in Hindi and Kannada language would be screened in these theatres. Single-screen cinema was the only concept that existed back then. To buy tickets over the counter after beating long queues was part of the excitement of movie-watching. Prabhakar would often go to the movies with his friends to immerse himself in the magic of black and white cinema with superstars like Dev Anand, Dilip Kumar and Raj Kapoor, the famous Bollywood actors of the 1950s and 60s.

One such movie that was released in 1960 and became a hit, was one of the not-to-be-forgotten-anytime-soon movies,

Mughal-E-Azam. The movie was the undying love story of Prince Salim and a courtesan Anarkali. This movie to date is still labeled as one of the evergreen releases from Bollywood. Anarkali was played by Madhubala, the most beautiful actress of the time. Every adolescent boy was in love with her and longed to see her beauty and inimitable grace on screen. Prabhakar managed to get tickets to this movie, but only for a late evening show that was until 10 pm. The movie had carried the boys into a different world, of royal settings, eternal love, impeccable dialogues, mesmerizing music and of course left them sighing as they spoke in words and expressions about their beautiful Madhubala even after the movie was over. It was only when they stepped out into the darkness of the real world, literally, did they realize it was too late in the night. Prabhakar stopped walking for a few seconds, as though he lent all his energy to his thoughts that were racing to find excuses to deliver to the elders who received him at this late hour at home. He made up one soon, though not very convincingly, and headed towards home but unfortunately did not get a chance to use it. He knocked at the door and waited for a long time. No one answered. His uncle had commanded the entire family to not let Prabhakar into the house that night. His doubts about Prabhakar going wayward were only strengthened beyond question that day. Prabhakar had to learn a lesson. It was his uncle's indisputable decision. That night, Prabhakar had to bear with both the cold weather and the coldness of his family.

The golden years of Prabhakar's childhood were filled with such memories. Little did he know then that just like the climax and anticlimax of a movie, the good days of childhood would end soon and fate was around the corner to meet him with many challenging twists and turns in the years to come.

Rocky Road to Adulthood

Untimely Death

The year was 1962 and Prabhakar was in grade 11 and like any boy of that age, he was beginning to visualize his dreams and preparing to achieve his future goals. It was mid-morning and Prabhakar was attending a wedding ceremony, when suddenly, he received the news of his father suffering a heart attack. At that time, Gopalaswamy was posted at Byadagi station and while on duty, he had coughed up blood. Byadagi is a small town in central Karnataka, and in those days, was underdeveloped with just basic amenities. There was no hospital where he could be taken to in such an emergency. His colleagues thought it was best to inform his brother, Taranath, to pick him up soon and take him to Hubli for treatment. As they waited anxiously for Taranath to arrive from Hubli, Gopalaswamy's condition began to worsen. They could not wait any longer and decided to send him on a train to Hubli as that would probably save time. However, Taranath had already boarded the train from Hubli and they missed each other. When Gopalaswamy arrived in Hubli, he was taken to the hospital by the railway employees stationed there. However, the strenuous journey had worsened his condition and it was too late and he did not survive. By the time Taranath boarded the next train back to Hubli to meet his brother after all the confusion, it was too late, and he had to meet his deceased brother at the mortuary. He felt helpless and pained with this sudden and untimely loss of his brother. But fate had its way, as always. Gopalaswamy's job as a station master and his erratic and acquired lifestyle had taken a toll on him. Long working hours, late night shifts and smoking had not taken long to prove harmful to his health. At the age of 37, Gopalaswamy was gone, leaving behind a young widow with five children: Prabhakar, Somashekar, Girish, Rukmini, and Harish. His mortal remains were arranged to be sent to his family and arrived at Mysore for the last rites. This was the first twist in Prabhakar's life, and many more turns awaited him.

Jayasheela Rao

Gopalaswamy was the sole breadwinner of the household. In the olden days, patriarchy was much observed and the roles of men and women in the family were almost pre-set and followed as a rule. The man was the designated earning member and would fend for the family, sometimes even travelling or staying elsewhere to earn his living. The woman was the caretaker of her home and family, and she stayed home to nurture the children. The roles were so defined that men were educated enough to earn a decent job whereas the women were barely educated but were efficiently trained in household skills.

Gopalaswamy, during his tenure in the Railways, had opted to invest in Railway Provident Fund instead of the Pension Fund. This meant that the family would be paid a lump sum amount on his retirement or his death. As per this rule, Gopalaswamy's family was given an amount of 6,000 rupees after his death. Relatives poured in to offer their condolences and to accommodate this huge influx of people and to perform the rituals of the final rites, Prabhakar's uncles rented a *choultry*, a big expensive hall. The *choultry* was rented for two weeks to perform the 14-day ritual and a whopping 5000 Rupees were spent on it! Little sense did it make that Gopalaswamy's uncles made such a thoughtless decision to spend a huge amount on the rituals, leaving behind only 1000 rupees for the family that was now facing a bleak future.

After the last rites were performed, Prabhakar could feel the burden of the world weighing heavily on his shoulders, both emotionally and financially. Being the oldest and being a man, he was undoubtedly expected to take over the responsibilities from his father. He wondered how he would feed his mother and siblings. At the tender age of 17, Prabhakar grew up overnight to be an adult in the family.

Amid this confusion and acceptance of the sudden change, Prabhakar received a letter from his father's distant cousin in Bangalore, Jayasheela Rao. The letter seemed like any other, offering condolences to Prabhakar and family. But no, there was something more that was soothing to Prabhakar's turmoil of the prior few days. Jayasheela had advised in his letter that Prabhakar should not give up his studies. He had heard that Prabhakar was a very diligent and a smart student and strongly felt that under no circumstances should he ever give a thought about discontinuing college. To support this strong advice, Jayasheela also promised that he would be available to reach out to for anything, anytime. For Prabhakar, who was drowning under the burden of responsibilities and felt orphaned with no one to guide or mentor him, this letter came as a blessing. Jayasheela's words were so inspiring and gave Prabhakar inexplicable strength and direction which turned out to be the biggest inspiration for him. His relatives however continued persuading him to apply for a job in the Railways. "You will be offered a job on compassionate grounds, Prabhakar. After all your father has served in the railways for long and even risked his health to fulfill his duties. You should easily be offered at least the position of a second division clerk", they unanimously declared. While these discussions filled the household, Prabhakar's thoughts oscillated between both the paths that were laid before him. One, continue his father's service even before he could finish his studies and lead the same kind of life that he had, away from family. The other was to educate himself and take on a new journey.

The words of encouragement from Jayasheela Rao kept resonating in his mind and he started to truly believe that he could be a successful person someday if he continued his education. However, he did not overlook the need of the hour either. He decided that the only way he could earn for his family was to conduct tuition classes for children, while he continued his studies. He was confident of his decision and determined to make it work for all. After considerable effort he found four families who wanted their children tutored. He chose an early morning and late evening schedule to accommodate the tuitions of all the children and used the day to attend his college. Every morning he would set out for work on his bicycle, early enough to welcome the sun rising to light up the eastern sky. He would enjoy the ride through almost empty roads and pass by fields where bullocks were starting their work too, ploughing the fields among glistening rows of crops. The lady of the first house that he visited was kind enough to provide him breakfast as he taught her kids. Her generous words *"thindi thogolappa"* signaling him to have breakfast were the sweetest to Prabhakar's ears. He would forever remember that one hot meal in the morning that kept him going through the day until his evening tea. It was indeed the tastiest and most treasured. Prabhakar would continue tuitions in the evenings as well in two other houses. Some days, he would be offered snacks and tea in those houses and he would skip dinner at home. On other days, he would return home famished and have dinner. Dinner was usually leftovers from his uncles' homes. Regardless of what was cooked - rice, *rasam*[16] - everything would be mixed so there was enough volume to feed his mother, siblings, and himself. Prabhakar felt content that he was able to provide whatever little for his family and with the support of others, they had the basic needs fulfilled - shelter, clothing, and food. Gratitude for this and all the hard work of the day gave him a good night's sleep each night.

Prabhakar was not deterred by life's harsh circumstances. His determination to study further only grew stronger, and over the next few years of struggling between tuitions, studies and looking after his family, Prabhakar graduated with a bachelor's diploma in science. His friends Murthy and Chandru went on to study in engineering colleges. Prabhakar could not have afforded such an expense. After he got his degree, he enrolled in AMIE, which was a technical training course. In other words, a poor man's engineering course. He finished his junior course and as a final step for completion, needed to enroll in practical training. To do this, he

---

[16] *rasam - traditionally prepared using kokum or tamarind juice as a base, with the addition of tomato, chili pepper, black pepper, cumin, and other spices as seasonings*

took up a job at the Java motorbike factory in Mysore. Thus, began the journey of his career.

Every day until then and even later, he was immensely thankful for the letter that had arrived just in time as a beacon of guiding light. Jayasheela Rao had made that difference in a young boy who stood helpless at a crossroad after the biggest tragedy of his life

F.K. Irani and the Java Factory

Prabhakar started his job as a Quality Inspector at the Java factory with great enthusiasm and energy. This was his first formal job related to the technical field he was trained in and he was looking forward to it, for both the money and the experience. The factory operated in two shifts. The early morning shift was from 6:00 am to 2:00 pm and the general shift was from 8:00 am to 5:00 pm. Prabhakar chose the early morning shift. He was still struggling to make ends meet and provide basic needs for his family. He was aware that he needed to work and earn as much as possible. So, he planned to work in the factory in the mornings and accommodate time for tuitions in the evenings. It worked well for him and the routine went on smoothly for years.

The factory was huge and employed many workers. The production units were always buzzing with the noise of machines that were operational full time and the occasional talk among the employees who also worked without any considerable breaks. The rules of the factory were stringent. The shifts were long, and sirens went off to announce lunch breaks and recess. The workers were expected to follow the timings strictly. To keep them motivated, there was an attendance bonus of 10 rupees per month for employees who were punctual. The salary of 80 rupees was given to those who had full attendance. Prabhakar adhered to all the rules of the factory and did his best to earn the bonuses too. But there were some rules of the factory that Prabhakar did not appreciate and soon his enthusiasm to work there began to fade.

Every day, the factory workers were frisked and checked to make sure they were not stealing parts of the machinery from the factory and selling them outside. No one was spared the search, and this was a strict instruction from the owner of the factory, Irani. Though it was not his actual name, he was referred to as Irani because he was from Iran. Prabhakar did not like this process. Somehow his ego was hurt every time he was searched. His pride and dignity in his education and qualification as a graduate did not make him comfortable with any action that would question his honesty. However, he consoled himself by trying to understand that this was a requirement of the job. He also knew that he needed the money and could not be upset with the rules. But this was not all. In the next few days, Prabhakar was unpleasantly exposed to many other realities of the work in the manufacturing unit and the working conditions in the factory.

It was not uncommon to hear screams or cries of pain from machine operators who were prone to cuts on their fingers or fatal injuries on their hands while at work. Prabhakar later learned that these accidents could be largely prevented through security locks in the machines, but they were deliberately not used because it would slow down the production work. "How could laborers be treated so casually? Did the management not feel the guilt of such inhuman treatment and bloodshed on his hands?", Prabhakar often thought, helpless and frustrated. He did not know that there was more in store for him to experience and not all of those would be pleasant. There would soon be a turning point too in his life.

In electrical and mechanical trades and manufacturing, each half of a pair of mating connectors or fasteners is conventionally assigned the designation male or female. The female connector is generally a receptacle that receives and holds the male connector. There are exact specifications of manufacturing the male and female connectors, so that they fit and connect well once they are manufactured. The factory manufactured both the male and the female spare components. The workers followed the specifications from the drawings of engineers and the idea was to fit the connector to the receptor and sell it.

The early morning shift was buzzing with activity that fateful day. It was the last week of the month and the challenge was to meet the production count before the month ends. The demand for the manufactured units were very high that month and the workers were busy working to meet the target. In the rush to produce more numbers and perhaps due to working overtime, they accidentally produced 500 pieces of male connectors with a small mistake in measurement on that day. The worker had made a mistake in the setting when using the slide calipers. Prabhakar was doing the inspection at the time. When he noticed this mistake, he referred to the diagrams and did a critical analysis. He figured out that instead of wasting the 500 pieces, if he can alter the machine setting to a small change so that the female receptor also aligns with the same measurement as the male connector produced, he could make it work. He looked for the production manager on the floor to ask him for permission to attempt the alteration of the setting and divert the wastage. He did not find the manager and so he went ahead and executed the specification. On his instruction, the unit set to work. The floor manager came in later and found out regarding the production attempt led by Prabhakar, using the altered specification. He was furious and did not wait to listen to Prabhakar's explanation of his idea. Instead, he insulted Prabhakar and asked him to meet him at the office of the Head of Manufacturing facility.

Prabhakar felt very humiliated and dejected. "I was only trying to be helpful to the company by diverting a financial loss. Do I deserve this treatment in front of all the employees?", Prabhakar thought with a sigh as he walked towards the office of the Head. However, the Head did not react on impulse. He patiently listened to the complaint from the floor manager and then turned to Prabhakar to hear his side of the story. "Prabhakar, why did you make the changes in the specification? How will it help us? Can you explain?" he asked attentively. Prabhakar felt a moment of relief. He took a deep breath and laid out the situation to the Head. He then walked back to the production floor with renewed confidence and perfectly matched the male and the female connector. The Head was very impressed with the successful demonstration. He smiled and then turned to the floor manager with a frown and a disagreeable nod, "Look! Prabhakar's solution has saved us today. Learn to listen and observe instead of being impulsive about complaining against a person!" He patted Prabhakar on his back and complimented him for his wise thinking and his timely solution.

Prabhakar should have been happy after this appreciation, but somehow, he felt a lack of interest in the job. It was the third week of the month. His only motivation was that he would collect his salary along with the bonus of 10 rupees for perfect attendance in another week. The following week, he felt very restless and preoccupied. His mind raced with thoughts of his uncertain future. He felt trapped in the job. He had no mentor or guide to speak to. His thoughts were jumbled, and he felt alone, with no one to advise or give him solace. He was the oldest in the family and the main breadwinner. Who could he share his concerns with? Prabhakar's days and nights moved on with these thoughts.

It was the 28th day of the month. Prabhakar woke up to the usual brightness of dawn not knowing then that the day was going to be unusual and the darkness of dusk would bring a new twist to his life. Early that morning, Prabhakar took his bicycle out to head to the factory and did not notice that it had a flat tire. He rode on until the bicycle went out of control in just a few minutes of the ride. He had to travel eight kilometers every day to reach the factory and with this mishap, there was no chance of him getting there on time. Neither did he have the time to get the punctured tire fixed. He would lose the bonus of 10 rupees after a whole month of punctual attendance and hard work!

He did not give up easily, though. He picked up the bicycle and ran as fast as he could. "I can still try and make it on time and earn my 10 rupees if I run fast", he thought with determination. As he ran towards the railway crossing, the train track gate was closing in. If he did not make it to the other end of the track before the closing, he would be late to the factory. Sweating profusely, he continued to run but tripped on a stone and fell. When he got up to make a dash to the railway gate, it was too late. The gates were closed. His spirits sank. He would be stuck for the next 15 minutes and he knew he would not make it to the factory on time. All his effort went in vain. As he watched the passing train helplessly, something snapped in him and he let himself fall to the ground as though a burden weighed heavily down on him. He sat on the pavement and watched the train pass by near the foothill of Chamundi Hills. He looked at the train and far beyond at the horizon and started to cry. He bawled loudly, letting out all his pain. He did not know why he was crying. Was it the job that had made him see so much blood and the workers in pain, or the insults that he had to bear? Or was it simply because he was going to lose the 10 rupees after an entire month of reaching the factory on time? He did not know. He did not have a shoulder to cry on, but the tears flowed. The hills seemed to bear his pain and lent him the shoulder he was missing so he could cry.

After the train passed, he wiped his tears and got up, dusted his knees, and limped to the factory gate. He met his friend outside the gate. He had decided by then that he was going to quit his job. He met the Head and put forth his decision. The Head was surprised to hear this. Somebody had mentioned to him about the woes of Prabhakar's family and he knew the boy would have no money if he gave up his job. He tried to convince Prabhakar to rethink but Prabhakar had made up his mind. He did not know where he would go next or how he would feed his family, but he just knew he wanted to quit, and he did. He felt a strange sense of relief as he walked out. He asked his friend to loan him two rupees. He went to a hotel nearby and ordered four *idlis*[17]. He wiped his eyes, sat down to eat, savored the idlis, and walked back home. His stomach was full and satiated, but he felt empty and tired. The darkness of dusk was arriving, leading him to yet another path of uncertainty that he had to tread. One that would not even show him light the next dawn.

---

[17] *idlis - steamed rice cakes*

Sundar

Prabhakar's life had slowed down after he quit his job at the Java factory. It was not because of the better conditions, but due to a bleak future with no hope of light yet, even at the end of the tunnel.

Prabhakar and his family continued to live off meagre meals and their states of mind were no better than the creaking wooden cots and beds of their home that were showing signs of wear and tear under duress. The vessels that were sure to be emptied every night seemed to speak volumes about the emptiness that took Prabhakar to bed every night, with only hope and prayer for a better tomorrow.

It was amid these difficult times that Prabhakar had a chance meeting with one of his teachers. The teacher listened to Prabhakar's life story and advised him to pursue B.Ed. Bachelor's in Education, a qualification that would guarantee him the job of a teacher. He also said that this course would earn him a stipend while he was studying, because the course curriculum involved practice teaching in schools.

Prabhakar took the advice of his teacher and got admitted to the B.Ed. course. He completed the course successfully. His first success as a teacher though was a life-changing one for his friend, Sundar. Sundar worked as a Class D officer in the Railways and due to some unfortunate circumstances, had failed to complete his SSLC (10th grade). Prabhakar encouraged him to complete his SSLC through correspondence and tutored him to prepare for the exam. In those times, passing SSLC was a great achievement and a surefire way for getting promoted to higher levels in a job. For Sundar too, this proved soon enough. As soon as he completed his 10th grade under the able and personal guidance of Prabhakar, he was promoted as a Class C officer. His joy knew no bounds. His once stagnant future had moved on to newer and better opportunities. Indeed, Sundar felt deeply indebted to Prabhakar and to express his gratitude to his friend-teacher-guide, gifted him a coat. That was Prabhakar's first coat which he treasured and wore for all his B.Ed. seminars thereafter. The black coat, ironically, had dispelled some darkness from Prabhakar's life and was his first symbolic success as a teacher. Sixty years later, the coat still hangs with pride in Prabhakar's closet.

The Eligible Bachelor

By the time Prabhakar was 21, he had grown into a handsome young man and was undeniably the town's most eligible bachelor. His dark curly hair and fair skin enhanced his looks, only to add more value to his qualification and success through all the struggles in his life. While many of the village folk eyed him as a potential groom for their daughters, it was one of the close family members who had already reserved Prabhakar and thought he was right in doing so! His maternal uncle Venkatesh *mava* had decided on his own to have his daughter married to Prabhakar. He would throw hints now and then about it, but Prabhakar would always casually brush the proposal aside. Venkatesh *mava* was not one who would give up easily though. He found ways to pressurize Prabhakar. He thought of the best plan that would drive him to be cornered into this commitment. He took Prabhakar to his aunt, Kittamma, in Malavalli. There were other relatives too who lived in Malavalli and Venkatesh *mava* knew it would be easy to convince Prabhakar with a larger number of people to support his decision.

Kittamma lived in a modest mud house. It was painted white with four blue pillars in the front porch that symmetrically formed the structural support for the house. The house looked very bare, lacking even the most basic of amenities. Two old wooden chairs graced the verandah and were offered as seats to older guests. To greet and host other visitors, mats were spread out on the floor.

It was one fine afternoon and the family had gathered under the cool, sheltered porch of Kittamma's humble abode to discuss Prabhakar's marriage. They all knew the reason for the gathering and had already supported Venkatesh *mava's* decision unanimously. They were also sure that Prabhakar would be very happy and agree to the proposal. In whispers, the family spoke about how Prabhakar owed his uncle a lot and he could 'repay' him best in this way. Everyone seemed pleased with this alliance.

Prabhakar could sense the excitement around him. He began to feel a little uneasy. He did not want to marry his uncle's daughter. He had never envisioned his uncle or her daughter with such intentions. Yes, he did owe Venkatesh *mava* a lot for all his support through the difficult days. He had grown up in his house and always had deep love and respect for him. However, this alliance was something he just could not accept with his mind and heart. He knew his decision would impact many relations and create bitterness in the joint family. But he had to refuse, and he had to do it now.

Finally, the formal proposal was placed before him. There was silence and Prabhakar felt innumerable pairs of eager eyes and attentive ears shifting in his direction. He did not pause long before he uttered a firm "No", to the unpleasant surprise of his uncle and all the others gathered there. The guilt of his decision weighed heavily on Prabhakar as he walked away leaving Venkatesh *mava* seething in anger and disbelief.

The family dispersed soon after and Venkatesh *mava* left for Mysore immediately. He did not bother to ask Prabhakar to join him. To his dismay, Prabhakar realized that his uncle had left him behind, and he did not have enough money to return alone! He had only two rupees which was not enough to travel from Malavalli village to Mysore. He knew it was not appropriate to ask Kittamma for money because of her bleak financial condition. Hence, Prabhakar had to make a quick calculation. He could travel from Malavalli town to Mysore with the money he had. So, he walked six kilometers to the town, from where he could board a bus to Mysore.

The walk was long and lonely. Prabhakar had come to the village with his uncle but was heading back alone. He knew that his decision would not be received well by anyone and that he had to face everyone's wrath once he was back home. Venkatesh *mava* would never forgive him and Prabhakar knew that he had to live with this guilt for the rest of his life.

New Headmaster of Bekkalale

After he completed his B.Ed. course, Prabhakar was deputed to his first job in a village called Bekkalale, which is a few kilometers from Mysore in the Maddur-Mandya district. It was a typical village with lush green fields and houses with cool verandahs and cattle sheds. Most of the village folk were farmers and toiled in the fields to earn their meagre income. Colorful deities of gods and goddesses that were believed to protect from enemies, ill-luck, and natural calamities adorned the village. Interestingly, cats are worshipped in this village and the practice continues, true to the name Bekkalale, *Bekku* meaning cat in *Kannada*[18].

The village had one school, and kids from nearby villages also attended the high school in Bekkalale. Schools were limited to a few villages during those days, and children would walk or cycle miles to the nearest school. The school building wore an outdated look with the walls cracked in incorrigible patterns

---

[18] *Kannada - Language spoken in the state - Karnataka in India*

that yielded visual pathways. The roof was chipping off unapologetically, as if tired from years of serving over the head and the floor below was bare and cracked just as the heels of innumerable aspirants. The rusted, old school bell diligently continued its duty of timekeeping. This certainly was not Prabhakar's dream job and for a young man like him who was starting his career, a better scene would have been more motivating. However, Prabhakar did not complain. As with many other times in his past, he could not afford to do it. The road ahead was still too long. But it was certainly brighter.

Prabhakar was assigned Grade 10 and there were 24 children in his class. All the 24 had failed to clear the examination the previous year and were eagerly waiting for their new teacher to coach them and prepare well enough to pass the forthcoming exam. As Prabhakar began his interaction with the class, he realized that there were a lot of gaps in their knowledge and as a first step, the children needed basic concepts to be reinforced. He could foresee a huge effort that needed to be put in by both the teachers and the students, to inch forward. "It would be a miracle if we can cover the entire syllabus. To get the children to pass in the examinations is yet another challenge!" Prabhakar thought introspectively. However, he set forth undeterred and decided to give his best to this situation as well.

Prabhakar began his work by trying to understand the root of the problem first. He called for all the children and their parents to meet him. He listened to their woes patiently. He sat back to hear their complaints of poor teaching in the previous years, nodding attentively all the while. Once they finished pouring out their concerns, he leaned forward and spoke in a confident tone. "Do not worry! This year will be different, and your children will fare better, okay? I take complete responsibility for that." He convinced them and brought his palm down on the table as if in a gesture of promise. The parents were indeed happy to hear this and had complete faith in the new headmaster. They dispersed with smiling faces, whispering to each other in relieved tones. He also had a meeting with all the teachers to hear their side of the story. The high school teachers complained that the middle school had a broken system and that was where the failure began. "Sir, the middle school teachers just let the students pass without assessing them properly. That is the problem. We get a class full of students who do not even know the basics. You tell us, sir, how can they improve? It is so difficult, sir!", they alleged with total disappointment. Middle school teachers in turn had the same complaint against the elementary school teachers.

Prabhakar realized he had a huge task at hand as the headmaster and began thinking about ways to address the problem. First, he formed an association of teachers and invited all the B.Ed. professors and the Dean of Mysore University to preside over meetings. In these meetings they discussed changes to their teaching and approach methods. They were mentored and motivated to make a difference in the life of the students. Prabhakar then shifted focus to the students to give them their task. He challenged them to aim for better marks and gave them study schedules. They were required to be at school from 8:00 am to 4:00 pm, which were the regular hours. However, this would not end their day at school. A break of two hours was given after school hours and they had to regroup to take extra classes, based on the subjects they were weak in and had trouble coping with. Prabhakar's implementation of this academic rigor became the talk of the town and was much appreciated. The news travelled farther to reach Prabhakar's hometown. His uncle Shripathi *mava* heard of it and experienced renewed hope of his son Bhojraj passing his 10th grade. He sent him to Bekkalale without any further delay.

Prabhakar soon had many young lives to set right and this was just the beginning.

Not long after, Prabhakar's family in the village had a new addition. Venkatesh *mava's* son Puttrama also joined them.   As the members of the family increased, so did the number of mouths to feed. All of this with just one man's earnings. The villagers soon understood the struggle Prabhakar was going through to look after even the basic needs of his family. They were sensitive enough to help in any way possible by doing their bit. "The headmaster is doing so much to help our children, no? Why can't we also help his family in return? Let us do something...anything we can!", suggested a few villagers and the rest of them readily agreed in an affirmative chorus. They started providing vegetables, rice, coconuts and whatever they grew in their own farms and was available to them in abundance. They wanted to express their gratitude for the help their children were receiving, and this was an apt way of doing it. Soon an unconditional bond was developed between Prabhakar and the villagers. Prabhakar too did not leave any stone unturned in his effort to mentor the students. He stayed up late into several nights to prepare quizzes for the students. He adopted many such interesting learning methods for them apart from classroom lessons.

Prabhakar noticed the classrooms were very dirty. So, he undertook cleaning some of the shelves. There were chemicals that the class was supposed to use for the labs. He asked everyone to be careful while cleaning around it. However, one of the kids when trying to reach out to dust the upper shelf accidentally knocked the containers that had some chemical in it. The container broke spilling the liquid on the floor. The fumes consumed the classroom as Prabhakar evacuated all of them to safety. He realized upon inspection that it was liquid ammonia so old and expired that it would have been a hazard if he had used it in experiments. He had all the shelves cleaned. School supplies were scarce in village schools but that did not mean expired products deserved to be on shelves. With this incident, he warned the school authorities to not neglect the safety of the school.

Kids were slowly getting acclimated to the rigor and discipline set by their new headmaster. Attendance was good and his students never missed school. However, in one of the morning classes, as he took attendance Prabhakar realized he was missing his student from the nearby village. The student would cycle to school every day to attend his classes. By evening that day, villagers gathered near the school to tell him about the missing student. He was cycling to school that morning when a *Garuda,* an eagle dropped a snake on his head. The snake was venomous and bit the boy before the eagle swooped back and picked up the snake high into the sky. The nearest hospital was miles away and by the time villagers got him to the hospital the poison had spread, and the boy had succumbed to the snakebite. The news shocked Prabhakar but for the villagers it was not uncommon and Prabhakar was to learn as to why as days passed. He would witness big snakes slithering at the steps of his home or when walking on the paths. He wondered about village life and how folks romanticize life in a village. It was not easy to lead a life in the village. He wondered about the uncertainty of life and fate that does not spare anyone.

As Prabhakar was settling himself in, he became aware of the political situation in the village. Powerful landlords, Kalse Gowda and Bhadre Gowda were two brothers pitted against each other and they represented different political parties. Fights would suddenly erupt between the two parties. Prabhakar heard from the villagers that people from both parties would clash over trivial matters with violence and sometimes it would get bloody. The brothers would occasionally visit the school and Prabhakar would be cordial to both. Each of them would complain about the other. Prabhakar would just listen but was careful not to enforce any opinion. He would not agree nor disagree with anything that was said by either brother.

Once, when Prabhakar was returning from a trip to Mysore, he saw dozens of police cars outside Kalse Gowda's house. Prabhakar rushed to the house but was stopped by the inspector. He said "Nobody can go up the stairs. Who are you?"' Prabhakar explained he was the school headmaster and he knew Kalse Gowda very well and wanted to know if everything was alright with him. The inspector explained they were waiting for Kalse Gowda to come down. It had been hours since they had called out for Kalse Gowda. Prabhakar could see that the inspector was in fear. As he continued to talk, he said he did not know if people were armed upstairs. Prabhakar sensing all this convinced the inspector that he knew the landlord and would bring him down. When Prabhakar went upstairs he found Kalse Gowda sitting on the terrace smoking a beedi. Prabhakar approached him. "*Gowdre*", he requested "Why have the police come? Why aren't you coming down?" Kalse Gowda retorted, "This is the work of Bhadre Gowda. He sent for the police claiming his people were beaten. Election is around the corner so he must be doing this for publicity. If the inspector wants to question me, let him come upstairs. I have nothing to fear." He looked at Prabhakar once again, and said "*Meshtre*[19], why are you here? You should go home. This can get ugly soon." Prabhakar answered patiently, "It is not nice for the police to enter the premises of a house where your wife and children live. Let us go downstairs and resolve it with the police."

---

[19] *Meshtre - meaning teacher in Kannada*

The earnestness with which Prabhakar spoke was enough for Kalse Gowda and he came down with Prabhakar. Prabhakar managed to convince the inspector to give him a couple of days so he can mediate between the brothers to resolve this situation. The inspector was more than happy to hear this. Prabhakar sent for Bhadre Gowda and held a meeting. He reminded them that they were brothers and that they should be standing together regardless of their disagreements. The women of the households were the ones suffering. Their silent tears are not to be ignored. Generations would be impacted by these fights and the gaps would only increase. If the brothers could not reconcile, how would their children stand a chance to bridge the gap? Both the brothers were perhaps tired of the ongoing rivalry, their egos had prevented them from approaching the other. With Prabhakar as mediator, however, it became easy for them to reconcile. As Prabhakar continued, he said "*Maari habba* [20]is around the corner. Please celebrate it together." *Maari habba* is in fact celebrated as a mark of communal harmony in many villages. People from all religions, Hindus, and Muslims, set aside their differences and celebrate this festival together. With the reunion of the brothers, Prabhakar had won the hearts of the villagers. He was now one among them.

Prabhakar tried not to get distracted with these incidents and instead started to focus more on the students and their preparations for the upcoming exams. The students were gearing up well. Finally, the date of the examination arrived and teachers from all over the district arrived for the invigilation. These teachers were deputed to make sure no school cheated to

---

[20] *Mari habba – Celebration of Goddess Sridevi and during this festival a fair is organized for the participation all people in the village.*

help their students pass the exams unethically. Some teachers were known to be lenient enough to ignore the quiet sharing of answers through whispers and signals across the room. A few others would be sincere and strict. They would keep a watchful eye and stop any kind of communication during the scheduled exam time. Prabhakar was assigned to a class where his nephew Bhojraj was writing his exam. Prabhakar's eyes travelled across the room like a scanner and quietly conveyed a strict note to all the students in the room that he would not allow anyone to peep into neighboring answer sheets or talk in whispers. Bhojraj was disappointed. He had hoped to get help on some of the questions from his friend across the bench but Prabhakar's eyes were smarter and sharper than he thought. The classroom had pin-drop silence. Bhojraj had lost all hope and gave up. So did a few others like him.

A few months later, just before the 10th grade results were announced, Prabhakar received a letter from K.S Venkatramaiah, who Prabhakar knew as K.S.V was the guardian and brother-in-law of Rathna. He had seen Rathna earlier in community gatherings and knew her to be beautiful and well educated. The letter was simple in which K.S.V asked if he would be interested in getting married to his wife's younger sister, Rathna. Rathna had a government job and he wanted to know if Prabhakar was interested in the alliance. Prabhakar was very excited to receive this proposal. He was very surprised that an alliance of a well-employed girl would even be offered to him. He decided to talk about it to his family. Exams were over and his mother and siblings had left earlier to Mysore and he had planned to join them for summer vacation.

Prabhakar was in an elated state of mind and was packing his bag to head to Mysore. He cleaned the house, washed all the vessels, and made sure any leftover food was emptied before he left the house. He only felt more energized after all the chores and picked up his luggage to head to the bus stop. There were two buses that would stop at Bekkalale - one at 6:00 am and the other at 6:00 pm. He had chosen to board the latter. It was 7:00 pm and well past sunset. Prabhakar looked eagerly through the dark night in hopes of seeing some sign of the bus arriving. He wondered if the bus had broken down on its way and decided to wait longer. He glanced at his watch time and again. It was 8:30 pm and there was still no sign of the bus. Prabhakar started to feel pangs of hunger. He realized in despair that there was no food left at home. Neither was there any hotel in the village where he could buy himself something. He felt his spirits drain. The hunger, thirst, long wait, and his sinking spirit gave way to a serious thought. How could he bring a young bride into such a village? How would she start her new life in a place so forsaken?

His mind was suddenly filled with doubts and questions. This was not a suitable place to raise a family. There was no sign of good life or basic comfort here and, no promising future. Prabhakar heaved a deep sigh, rose to his feet, and headed back home. His footsteps were heavy and slow-paced. He felt the familiar pain as he once again was on the path of uncertainty. He reached home after what seemed like a long journey from the bus stop. It was very dark, and the path back home had no streetlights. Prabhakar had not carried a flashlight with him since he had not anticipated the bus not to show up. The night was getting louder with crickets chirping, the birds had gone quiet but the slithering sounds in the bushes and frogs croaking away filled the night. The fireflies lit up along the fields seemed to be guiding Prabhakar as he made his way back home. He dropped his bag and hit the bed. He slept hungry that night, feeling empty in every way. Once again, he had decided to quit his job.

Prabhakar woke up the next morning, not feeling well rested. The day was new but brought with it was a surge of old doubts. He freshened up, picked his luggage, and headed to the bus stop in the hope of boarding the morning bus to Mysore. On his way, he stopped at the village headman's house to inform him of his decision to quit his job. Word spread rapidly and the entire village rushed to convince Prabhakar to stay back and revoke his decision. But Prabhakar politely refused, convincing them that he had no choice. The villagers were disappointed but had to accept his decision and let him move on. Prabhakar boarded the bus with a heavy heart and the villagers started crying and extending their hands into the window of the bus in their last attempt to stop him from going and begging him to stay back. Acknowledging all their emotions, Prabhakar checked his tears. He had earned so much love and respect. He now realized one of the greatest services to society was to be a good educator. As the bus moved, the morning breeze brought the memories of his short but fruitful stay at Bekkalale. He looked out at the passing scenes of the village through the window. The chapter had come to an end and he had empty pages after this to fill in. He closed his eyes as if to shut off the scenes, but his mind was not still. His thoughts seemed to race in sync with the moving bus.

That year, when the results were announced, the village folk were delighted and so were the school staff. All the 24 students had passed in their examination. However, there was one name on the list of failures - Bhojraj. Prabhakar's nephew had failed again and Shripathi *mava* forever blamed Prabhakar for it. The invigilator who did not let his son pass!

Ramnarasaiah

Back in his hometown in Mysore and jobless once again, Prabhakar was exploring new job opportunities. It was during this time that he met Prof. Nagappa, an old acquaintance, who informed him that there was a new initiative to encourage non-Hindi speaking population in universities to learn the language. An incentive that made the opportunity more lucrative was a scholarship of 100 rupees that one could avail if they opted to pursue the Masters, MA course in Hindi. The requirement for Hindi language professors would be on the rise soon and this would be a good option for Prabhakar who was desperately looking for a job. Prabhakar decided this was perfect for him. He could feed his family as well as study further and be assured of a job thereafter. He enrolled for MA in Hindi at Manasa Gangothri, the Mysore University. Not for the love of the language, but for the scholarship offered.

Prabhakar thus set out to earn his third educational degree from the prestigious and serene university campus in his very own hometown.

As a requirement for the completion of their course, the students were asked to present a seminar in their second year. Each student had to present a paper on a pre-assigned topic, and they would be evaluated by a panel of professors on various aspects such as content, presentation skills and confidence. The audience consisted of professors and students. Prabhakar had prepared good content for the presentation but was very nervous. He was not confident of talking in Hindi yet, and the language was unfamiliar to him for it was rarely heard or spoken in South India. To be able to speak for an hour was a big challenge for most students. But this was not optional and all of them had to face it with no exception!

For one last time before the seminar began, Prabhakar sat down outside the hall with his friend, Ramnarasaiah, to review his paper. He finished but was still feeling just as nervous. He got up to walk into the seminar room, his mind muddled with anxiety and Hindi words and sentences. As he rose, he heard a tear. It was his pants! A twig from the tree under which he had taken a seat had found its way to rip his pants into a considerably big tear.

Prabhakar's mind went blank. He stood staring at his pants and feeling lost. He had only 15 minutes to his presentation. How would he make it to the stage and face an audience in torn pants? If he did not make it on time and complete the presentation, he would fail and not get his degree. He would have to wait another year and he could not afford to lose time. There were so many dependencies on this qualification - a job, his family, and the new alliance he had just accepted. What would he do now? He froze with all these thoughts and his eyes welled up.

Ramnarasaiah who was standing by his side all the while, was witness to the whole incident. He realized the turmoil in Prabhakar's mind which reflected on his face unabashedly. He lost no time and grabbed Prabhakar by the hand. He pulled him onto his bicycle and without uttering a word, he started to ride. Prabhakar was still dazed but trusted that his friend was doing something for his good. About two kms away, he stopped his bicycle in front of a tailor shop. He signaled to Prabhakar to get off and hurriedly placed the cycle on its stand. Wiping his forehead to clear the sweat, he rushed towards the tailor. In between gasps, he quickly explained to him about the pant and, pointing to the tear, he requested the tailor to stitch it up as fast as possible. The tailor looked at the tear and then threw a quick glance at the two men. He understood the urgency with no further explanation and pushed aside all the things from the top of the tailoring machine to make space. He was fast at his work and within a few minutes, Prabhakar's pants were repaired. Ramnarasaiah thanked him profusely and pulled Prabhakar onto the bicycle once again and rode off as fast as he could, as the tailor looked on with a smile.

Prabhakar arrived in the seminar hall five minutes later than the scheduled time. He wiped his face with a handkerchief and asked to be excused for his late attendance. He explained that a small accident had prevented him from reaching on time and went on to start his presentation. After he finished, he was applauded with a standing ovation from the professors. Prabhakar was elated beyond words. He stood there acknowledging every clap and every praise wholeheartedly. He had faced the test of fate once again and triumphantly stood tall and unflinching.

In all this relief and joy, he did not forget who had helped him through. If not for Ramnarasaiah that day, Prabhakar would not have been saved from the challenging situation. He was indeed indebted to him.

Years later, Prabhakar met his dear friend and reminded him of the incident and how he had been his timely savior. Ramnarasaiah chuckled in delight and they clinked their by-2 coffee cups. By-2 coffee is a term used among friends to share a cup of coffee. They shared the coffee along with laughter and memories of good old days.

Dreams and Ambitions

Dr. Venkatesh

Bangalore,1972. Prabhakar had completed his MA in Hindi and his stint of two years at Manasa Gangothri was enriching, with both learning as well as teaching experience. His hard work and determination were highly appreciated by all his professors. He had developed a close bond with them, both academically and personally. Most of these professors were already familiar to him and supportive of Prabhakar's focus on work and diligence. They had been part of the association that Prabhakar had formed during his short, yet fruitful period of work at Bekkalale. He had continued to tutor students during his MA as well, mostly extending his services to the professors'

children. Over the years, Prabhakar had proven to be a leader, motivator, and an excellent teacher. All this was noticed and duly acknowledged by the teaching community.

Prabhakar was waiting for the right opportunity to find a suitable job that would set the track for his teaching career. Around the same time, Dr. Venkatesh, the Head of Department of Hindi in M.E.S College, Bangalore, had reached out to Dr. M.S. Krishnamurthy in Mysore asking if there were any good candidates to join his department as a lecturer. Dr. Krishnamurthy could not think of anyone but Prabhakar to be the right candidate and mentioned his name without hesitation. Prabhakar was asked to send his application for the job and attend an interview thereafter. One day prior to the interview date, he boarded a train to Bangalore, his next destination.

Prabhakar's old school friend Chandru was in Bangalore at the time, pursuing his studies at the prestigious Tata Institute. Since Prabhakar was new to the city, Chandru accompanied him to the college for the interview. M.E.S College was one of the most reputed colleges and was ranked among the top junior and degree colleges. The structure was an old and aesthetic stone building and rightly projected the impression of an institution that valued academic rigor. The college was known to admit only the best of students and securing admission there was the dream of every student and a goal set by every parent.

Prabhakar entered the college building with mixed feelings of hope and anticipation. After being asked by the security guard what the purpose of his visit was, Prabhakar replied, "Interview." The security guard nodded and said, "First floor," pointing diagonally upwards in a direction across the quadrangle. He seemed to have done this exercise many times that morning. Prabhakar walked in, taking a quick glance at the college premises before he headed to the stairs that led to the first floor. He felt a rush of uncertainty as he saw a huge turnout of candidates, waiting to be interviewed for the same job. There were at least 50 candidates for the post. *Will I stand a chance among all these candidates? They must be more experienced than me,* he thought to himself, from the look of some of them. He took a seat and quickly brushed his doubts aside. He was prepared to do his best and would get the job if he deserved it, he convinced himself.

The interview lasted for 30 minutes. Prabhakar was extremely confident of himself and the panel did not miss this trait as they placed their questions before him. He was completely honest with his answers and at ease with those that he did not know and politely apologized for not answering them. He finished the interview to the best of his ability and thanked the panel before he walked out. He took the train back to Mysore later that day and waited eagerly for the results of the interview in the days to follow.

After his visit to Bangalore, Prabhakar often thought of the city. He was impressed with the dynamic pace of the city as compared to the sleepy town of Mysore and other small towns that he had always lived. He dreamed of getting the job at M.E.S College and settling into a new and improved lifestyle in the big city. He eagerly waited to hear good news. Meanwhile, he received a job offer from a B.Ed. Teachers' college for the post of a lecturer. He was not too keen to take up the job as he knew it would involve teaching mostly senior teachers who had taken up the course to improve their earning capacity. Most of them would be just a few years short of retirement and Prabhakar at 21 would be their teacher! He did not relish the idea. Moreover, the pay scale at M.E.S College was more enticing. He continued to wait for a positive response and hoped for a miracle.

A fortnight had passed without any news from the college. Prabhakar began to lose hope and almost gave up on his dreams of the job and the city. His despair was evident and sensing this, his laundromat friend Raju suggested, "Why don't you go to Bangalore directly and check the results of the interview? I think you should." Thrusting a 10-rupee note into Prabhakar's hands, he added, "Take this with you". Raju knew well that he would not have the money to travel. This remained a debt forever, as Prabhakar was not able to repay Raju who left the town soon after.

So, it was with 10 rupees in his pocket that Prabhakar embarked on his journey to Bangalore. It was a Saturday when he arrived at the college premises. He headed straight to the office to make his enquiry. The manager sitting across the counter seemed to be busy catching up on his work to wind up the week. He noticed Prabhakar and stared at him for a long minute before he looked back at his work desk and asked without care, "Who are you? What do you want?" Prabhakar explained that he was one of the candidates who had attended an interview a few days back and was here again to know if he had cleared it. The manager stopped his work and looked up. He removed his reading glasses and rose from his seat. "So... you are Prabhakar?!" his voice raised now, in an unmistakably irritated tone. "How many letters do we send you? Today is the first day of duty for the new candidate to join. You were the selected candidate! Why did you not accept the offer? The job will now be offered to the second candidate in line since you did not show up all these days!", he exclaimed.

Prabhakar stood frozen. He had not received any letter! He stood there explaining his situation and fumbling for words, trying to convince the manager to understand his situation. As he was talking, Prabhakar felt a nudge on his shoulder. He turned around and saw Dr. Venkatesh. Prabhakar had been introduced to him briefly at the interview panel. Dr. Venkatesh was a medium-built smart man. He was dressed in a perfectly tailor-made crisp suit and neatly polished shoes. He wore the look of a professor and carried an air of confidence around him as he walked upright. He held out a handwritten letter. Prabhakar took the letter and as he read through the brief content, he felt relieved. It said, 'I am reporting to duty as of this date' and below was a line for signature. As Prabhakar smiled in gratitude, Dr. Venkatesh asked him to sign the letter and that was it. Prabhakar had the job now! As far as reporting to duty on the first day was concerned, Dr. Venkatesh walked Prabhakar down the corridor until they stopped in front of a classroom. He handed him a duster and a few chalk pieces and pointing to the classroom, said, "That is the second year B. Com class. You go in and this will be your first class to show that you reported to duty today". Prabhakar was taken aback. His mind went blank and his head was spinning. Too much had transpired too soon. He did not even have time to prepare. Neither could he think of what to do or say now. He just followed the instructions and walked slowly into the classroom. The class was full and noisy, and the new face made the students even more excited and mischievous, creating more chaos.

The class was for an hour and Prabhakar had to keep the students engaged. He started by asking the names of the students. One shouted, "My name is Tiger!" Amongst giggles came another answer, "Zebra!" Soon to follow was another eager hand swung in the air accompanied by "I am Chimp!" Prabhakar understood what the class was intending to do but kept calm. He smiled and looked up at them and spoke in a sober tone. "Well...alright then. It looks like I am in the right place. I was supposed to find the zoo and here I am!" There was silence for a few seconds and then a burst of laughter from the entire class. The students had warmed up to Prabhakar instantly and he spent the hour familiarizing them. He also shared a little bit about himself and his life's journey. The hour passed soon, and the bell rang. Students gathered around him welcoming him to the college. Prabhakar was already feeling comfortable in the new place and in the new job.

Dr. Venkatesh was waiting for Prabhakar outside the classroom. He knew that Prabhakar did not have a place to go and so he took him to his house. The day was *Shraavana Shanivara,* an auspicious Saturday and according to tradition, Dr. Venkatesh' s mother and wife were more than happy to have a *Brahmachari* (bachelor) to feed dinner to that night. During dinner, Venkatesh informed Prabhakar that all the professors had unanimously recommended him for the job. His distant uncle, Jayasheela Rao, from whom he had received a letter after the demise of his father asking him not to give up his studies then, had also put in a word of recommendation to the steering committee. Unknown to Prabhakar, Jayasheela Rao had kept himself updated on the career path that Prabhakar had taken and when he learned that Prabhakar had applied to M.E.S College, he immediately sent his word of request for Prabhakar's selection to the Principal Prof. M.P.L Sastry. This recommendation from a distinguished journalist weighed much more than the word from a political leader whose candidate was the second-in-line for the job.

The universe comes together to help people who strive hard. This was true in Prabhakar's life. He always received help from strangers, passing acquaintances, friends and elders who were his well-wishers. All of this had always been timely, unexpected, and overwhelming. Prabhakar's mind was filled with these thoughts of gratitude as he spent the evening dining and talking with Dr. Venkatesh's family. He found that Dr. Venkatesh had a sense of humor. He spoke to the point and matter-of-factly. He reflected the look of a self-made man who had attained his values through experience and had a sensitive approach to everyone and every situation around him.

Just having landed in a new city, Prabhakar did not have any idea where he would go next. He needed some time to find a place or to even visit his hometown to get his things. Until then he had to plan for his stay, food, and essentials. As Prabhakar finished his dinner and was preoccupied with the unknown, Dr. Venkatesh asked him to accompany him to a nearby building. This was a place that had been rented out to a few old students. On enquiring with the manager, they were informed that one room had shared space available for immediate occupancy. He requested Doddaiah, an occupant student, to accommodate Prabhakar for a short period. He also requested him to adjust the deposit and other rental payments until the following month. Doddaiah readily agreed and welcomed Prabhakar in. He handed him a straw mat, a pillow, and a blanket. So many things had happened so quickly, Prabhakar was too tired to process anything else and he fell asleep instantaneously that night.

Brahmana Angadi - The Shopkeeper

The next day, at the break of dawn Prabhakar woke up to the warmth of the sun's rays streaming through the window, accompanied by songs of birds. He looked around to get accustomed to the new surroundings he was in. The happenings of the previous day raced through his mind like passing scenes. Prabhakar stretched himself and sat up on the mat after what felt like a long and refreshing sleep. He could hear *Suprabhatham*[21], faintly playing from a distance, perhaps from a temple or from one of the houses in the residential neighborhood. As he freshened up, Doddaiah rushed in with a cheerful morning greeting and a beaming smile. "Coffee!", he announced, handing Prabhakar a steel tumbler of steaming, aromatic coffee. As Prabhakar accepted the coffee with gratitude, he thought and smiled to himself, *'What an eventful day yesterday was'?* At age 24, he had finally landed himself his dream job in the garden city of Bangalore.

Once the excitement of the previous day settled down, Prabhakar was jolted back to reality and his current situation. He realized that he had left his home with merely 10 rupees, of which he had already spent four rupees on meals and travel. He was left with just six rupees to survive the week. Prabhakar looked up at Doddaiah who was going about his chores to start the day. "Doddaiah, can you do me a favor, please? Will you be able to arrange a stove and a couple of vessels that I can use for a few days?" Without any thought, Doddaiah gave a quick reply "Oh, that would not be a problem at all! I have a small kerosene stove to spare, and a few vessels too. You can use them." Prabhakar was relieved and thanked Doddaiah profusely. He wished that someday he would be able to pay back or pay forward all the kindness he had received in life. Prabhakar finished the rest of his coffee that had turned lukewarm by then and casually groomed himself before walking out to the street.

The street was pleasantly calm and lined by quite a few big trees that offered good shade. Most of the houses had some empty space in front with a small garden. The old, but well-maintained structures gave an impression of them being ancestral homes. He walked past a few houses and then turned to head back to his room. He suddenly heard his belly roar with

---

[21] *Suprabhatham - It is a collection of hymns or verses recited early morning to awaken the deity in Hinduism*

hunger. His eyes fell on a grocery shop across the room that he was staying in. The shop was popularly known as *Brahmana Angadi*[22], the Brahmin's shop as he had heard someone mention. Most of the residents' grocery and essential needs were met by the stock in this shop. The owner of the shop seemed like a friendly neighborhood shopkeeper, who was content with his small business.

Prabhakar did not have enough money to buy himself groceries for the week. How could he even ask for a loan of provisions when he was visiting the shop for the first time and was a stranger to the shopkeeper? He continued walking towards the shop and as he was processing his thoughts for a solution, he greeted the shopkeeper pleasantly and asked for a banana and a cigarette. Even though Prabhakar was not a smoker, he had somehow concluded that shopping for a luxury item like a cigarette would project a good financial status. He handed the shopkeeper five rupees note - the only one that he had! The banana cost 25 paise and the cigarette, probably a rupee. The shopkeeper looked at the five rupees note and presuming that Prabhakar would have more money on him, requested "Do you have smaller change? It is only one rupee and 25 paise...so..." Prabhakar smiled at him confidently and pointed across the street to show him where he lived. "That should not be a problem. I stay right there, in a rented room. You can keep the change. I can always collect it later." The shopkeeper looked in the direction of Prabhakar's pointed finger and nodded silently in agreement. Hoping that his spontaneous idea had worked its way through to build trust, Prabhakar walked away with the banana and cigarette he had bought. The shopkeeper's eyes followed Prabhakar as he walked towards his room. He was still holding the five rupees note in his hand,

---

[22] *Brahmana Angadi - Brahmana represents a person's caste in Hinduism and Angadi means shop.*

feeling good about the trust he was bestowed with. After all, a first-time customer had believed him unconditionally. Prabhakar felt assured that the trust was now mutual. He ate the banana and his hunger was satiated for the moment.

A little while later, Prabhakar listed out a few essentials that he needed for cooking food for himself in the forthcoming week. He called out to a boy who was playing on the street and gave him the list, asking him to pass it to the shopkeeper. The list had only four items - rava[23], onions, kerosene, and cooking oil. The boy ran up to the shop and handed the piece of paper to the shopkeeper, pointing to Prabhakar who was watching from his room window, now waving his hand. He was hopeful that his 5-rupee note had built the bridge of trust strong enough to loan him some groceries. The shopkeeper acknowledged his wave and turned around to weigh a standard quantity of the items asked for and packed them quickly into a bag. He scribbled the cost of each item and the total on a piece of paper and dropped the bill into the bag.

The boy ran back with the bag and handed it to Prabhakar before returning to play. Prabhakar opened the bag and was happy to see that all the items were there and in considerably good quantity. The bill was for about 20 rupees, his first debt in the city.

Prabhakar lit the stove and made Upma[24] - a dish made from semolina. Upma is a south Indian dish that is easy to make and tastes like porridge but is of a thicker consistency. He sat down to eat his first meal and was satisfied with it. Prabhakar continued to make the same dish for all three meals

---

[23] rava - semolina
[24] upma - thick porridge made from semolina

every day, throughout the week. He had found a temporary solution for all his necessities: food, clothing, and shelter.

Prabhakar started his regular duties at college, understanding his work as well as the expectations of the management well. He studied the syllabus he had to cover and aligned himself with the functioning of the college. The week passed uneventfully, without problems.

Prabhakar had avoided going in the direction of *Brahmana Angadi* for the next few days. The day he received his first salary, he went up to the shopkeeper and said "Here sir, the amount I owe you. I had come by several times but...er...did not find you here." The shopkeeper was happy to receive his dues, but tilted his head with a slight frown and replied, "I was here all these days and the only time I step out is usually at lunch time...hmm...when did you come by?" Prabhakar broke into a sheepish grin and softly said, "Oh! Then that must have been the time I came by...your lunch time, you see." The shopkeeper accepted the answer and they exchanged greetings before Prabhakar walked away, feeling a little remorseful for lying. Many a time later in his life, Prabhakar wondered why he had not been truthful to the shopkeeper.

Fighting poverty and surviving in a society is like a duck swimming. The calm face of the duck does not show the rigorous paddling that happens underneath the water to stay afloat. Similarly, Prabhakar had not wanted the world to know of his difficulties. The lie was merely a mask for his struggles.

Vageesh and Bhoj

Prabhakar settled into a new apartment soon after. A few days later, he met Vageesh, his classmate from school. Vageesh was incidentally looking for a place to stay and they mutually decided that he could move in with Prabhakar as his apartment mate. Soon, Bhoj, a good friend of Vageesh, was also introduced to Prabhakar and the bachelor trio formed a bond of friendship, enjoying a lot of their leisure time together.

Prabhakar was an excellent cook and the boys often hung out together at mealtimes in the apartment to relish a delicious meal cooked by him. One such evening when they got together, Prabhakar was making *sambaar* with small onions and potatoes. *sambaar* is a popular south Indian stew of yellow lentils with vegetables usually eaten with rice. The aroma of the *sambaar* wafted through the air and filled the room. Vageesh and Bhoj exchanged a glance, as if in a moment of intoxication from the aroma and struck upon an idea. They decided to treat themselves to a bottle of beer as an accompaniment with their meal. They shared their idea with Prabhakar in great excitement and he smiled, acknowledging that it was a good idea. The two boys headed out, while Prabhakar got back to finishing the preparation of the meal.

Vageesh and Bhoj were back in a while with the beer. They decided to create an ambience of a five-star restaurant with dim lighting. They switched off all the lights and lit a candle. Happy with their own set up, they settled down and were about to make a toast when they heard a knock on the door. The boys looked at each other and hurriedly put the beer bottles away. Drinking and smoking were a taboo in society in those times and if anyone were seen taking pleasure from these vices, they would be labelled wayward for life. The boys surely did not want that to happen.

Prabhakar got up and rushed to open the door, wondering who could be visiting him at this hour. He opened the door to face an old man, probably in his late seventies or early eighties, with an intense look on his face. *"Namaskara...Meshtru idhaara?"* he asked, meaning "Is the teacher in?" Prabhakar knew that the old man was asking for him and introduced himself to be the *'Meshtru'*[25], quickly asking what the matter was. The old man was a stranger to Prabhakar, and he was impatient to know what the reason was that he had come in search of him all the way there. After all, the man had interrupted their party plan and Prabhakar wanted to finish the conversation soon and head back in to join the other two.

The old man said he was a relative of Prabhakar and he wanted to talk to him for a few minutes. Prabhakar nodded and ushered the old man outside rather than into the house. He did

---

[25] *Meshtru - Teacher in Kannada*

not want to disturb his friends and their party further. *What did this man want? How did he find him?* Prabhakar wondered. The old man continued to indulge in casual talk as he got down the stairs with Prabhakar following close behind. "How come there is no electricity in your room?", he asked. Prabhakar however was in no mood to answer this question or any other that he asked. He only wanted to know the intention of the old man's visit. So, he again stated, this time with an obvious tone of impatience, "Sir...I am Prabhakar. I am the one you came looking for. Now, can you please let me know who you are and what you want from me? Please?" The old man looked at him and smiled, unaffected by Prabhakar's tone and continued at his pace, just as any old man of his age would. He stated, "See...Prabhakar, you are a relative of mine..." and went on to justify his statement with an elaborate ancestral hierarchy of how they were related. "Your cousin's cousin... who married your aunt you know.... that aunt's...", he explained but Prabhakar lost the trail and the old man's voice just faded into the background of his thoughts. *Okay, but why did you want to meet me now?*

Finally coming to the point, the old man said "I came to invite you, Prabhakar. I want you to come home, so that we can welcome my father home, you see." Prabhakar was taken aback! This man is nearly 80 and a stranger and now he is talking of welcoming his father?! Before he could place his thoughts in question, the old man, as if reading his mind, clarified that the invitation was for a function where the yearly rites of his father would be performed. So that was what he meant by "inviting my father home". Prabhakar sighed and politely refused. He told the old man that he was not familiar with such rituals and would not be comfortable participating in it. Prabhakar convinced him to find someone else who could replace him.

The old man was not easily convinced. He tried to pressurize Prabhakar. Finally, when Prabhakar did succeed in convincing him, a whole hour had passed. He was relieved but also quite exhausted from the conversation. He went back to the room only to see that his friends had finished the beer and all the food by then. To this day, Prabhakar feels amused by the incident and Bhoj and he share a moment of laughter whenever they recollect it. Prabhakar also jokingly says that it may have been Rangamma *Akka's* clever game from heaven to make sure her grandson did not go wayward. Who else but her would be keeping an eye on him? How else would an eighty-year-old man whom Prabhakar had never heard of, or met earlier, mysteriously appear on his doorstep and disappear just the same way? The mystery remained unsolved, but Rangamma *Akka's* mission from heaven seemed to have been accomplished.

Iyengar

After Prabhakar had settled well in his job and in the new city, it was time for him to go to Mysore for further talks of his alliance with Nagarathna. He wanted to find a suitable house where they could stay after marriage. So, before heading to Mysore, his search began. He soon found an outhouse behind Malleshwaram Clubhouse for a monthly rent of 30 rupees and a deposit of 300 rupees. The house looked compact, neat, and well-ventilated.

Prabhakar moved into the new house and set it up with all the necessities. Vageesh, his roommate, moved in with him for the time being. The owner of the house was Iyengar, a friendly and accommodating person. Dressed in a traditional costume with a vertical *naama*[26] on his forehead, he gave the look of a typical Iyengar Brahmin at the first glance.

Iyengar took an immediate liking to Prabhakar and was overly concerned about his comfort in the house. Vageesh was very observant and noted this obvious bias towards Prabhakar. He was amused and clearly knew the intention of Iyengar's special interest in Prabhakar. He had two daughters of marriageable age and when Prabhakar mentioned that he was a lecturer, he had all the intentions that a father would upon seeing an eligible bachelor. Vageesh was surprised by the prompt and quick response with which Iyengar was fulfilling all Prabhakar's wishes. Prabhakar once mentioned that it was quite cold at night and with the roof being asbestos, it made it worse for him to sleep on the floor. The following day itself, Iyengar quickly arranged for a cot for Prabhakar to sleep comfortably on.

Vageesh knew there was something fishy behind the good intentions of the owner. His suspicions were confirmed when every morning, Iyengar would present himself at their doorstep with a steaming cup of coffee. He would bring only one cup of coffee and Vageesh was conveniently forgotten! A few nights in the new house brought them many unwelcome surprises too. They had visitors every night. Big rodents roamed freely in the house as if they were the actual occupants of the house and Prabhakar and Vageesh were generously allowed to share the space. Vageesh could not bear living in the house any longer and soon he packed his things and shifted back to their old room. Prabhakar was alone in the outhouse thereafter and had to bear with both, Iyengar and the rodents, all alone.

Prabhakar tried his best to adjust to the house. In a few days he realized it was in vain and the living conditions were not something that could be overlooked for long. He gave up

---

[26] *Naama - red vermillion on the forehead*

and pleaded with Vageesh to help him out of the difficult situation he had got into. He did not want to continue staying in that house but was hesitant to say the same to Iyengar. After all, Iyengar had been very kind and done more than any owner would have done for a tenant. So Prabhakar had only one solution.

The boys decided that they would vacate the house without informing Iyengar. One midnight, they decided to put their plan into action. They had packed most of their things and kept the bags ready. They gathered their luggage near the front door, slowly opened the latch and stealthily walked out, bidding a silent goodbye to their four-legged nocturnal friends. They sneaked out of the gate and went back to the old room where Vageesh had already returned to earlier. They were relieved that the plan was executed well and did not think how they would deal with what was to follow.

The next morning, Iyengar realized there was no one in the house when he went to greet Prabhakar with the morning coffee. He wondered where Prabhakar could have gone that early in the morning. He waited for a day or two but got anxious when there was no sign of Prabhakar even then. He went looking for Prabhakar in his college. Prabhakar was caught unaware when he saw Iyengar and he could not make up any story to cover up his act of disappearance. He awkwardly explained the situation to him and after much convincing, Iyengar agreed to return the deposit. Prabhakar had to pay for his actions though. He had to meet Iyengar every month for 10 months, before he could get back the entire deposit amount.

Rajarajeshwari

"*Akka*! They are all dry", Rathna declared, raising her voice to be audible enough to her sister from the terrace of the house. "Okay, collect them carefully and bring them down, Rathna!", Rajeshwari instructed loudly, tilting her head up towards the terrace. She had made rice papads and pickles and laid them out to dry in the sun. Rathna had helped her with the elaborate process of preparation of the items.

Rajeshwari, short for Rajarajeshwari, was Rathna's older sister. She was the matriarch of the family and was married off when she was 13 years old. In those times, child marriages were prevalent and were not questioned by law. In fact, their mother was married when she was only eight years old! Considering the average age that girls were married then,

Rathna, being all of 22 years was considered old and obviously a concern to her family for still being unmarried.

'Bhanu Krupa' was the name of the house where Rajeshwari lived with her husband in Mysore. It was a beautiful house with two spacious rooms, a big kitchen and an attic and was in the heart of the town just a minute away from the town circle called Vidyaranyapura circle. Bhanu Krupa was one of the most popular houses at the time in the area. The house always brimming with guests and activities, was easily identifiable to anyone in the area and locals would rightly point to the house in case folks stopped to ask for directions.

Rajeshwari was the commander-in-chief to Rathna and her other siblings. She fit the role perfectly; very generous but showed a strict side of herself when situations demanded. She had a unique personality and stood out like a queen, with an air of dignity around her. She was tall, beautiful and had the right blend of charm and command. She took most of the decisions for her family, with ease and thorough understanding. All the family members looked up to her and trusted her judgement and decisions.

Rajeshwari also fulfilled her role as a homemaker with equal commitment and care. She would ensure that everyone in the family, near and far, got their fair share of everything, be it love, pampering or goodies. As part of her yearly preparation of goodies, she would make a variety of pickles, papads[27] and snacks like chakli[28] and kodbale[29] which are fried snacks made from rice flour. It would take at least two months of preparation

---

[27] Papads- thin Indian wafers made from dried lentils or rice.
[28] Chakli – Spiral shaped savory snack with a spiked surface made from rice & lentils.
[29] Kodbale – Deep fried spicy and crispy rings made from rice flour.

to make the pickles. Raw mangoes, ginger and *maagliberu*[30], a root that is typically grown in the villages of Karnataka, had to be cut, marinated and spices added. For the *papads,* rice batter was spread out on a muslin cloth or on cane trays for it to be placed on the rooftop to dry in the sun. Rajeshwari made sure she prepared large quantities of each item for all her siblings and relatives. Once they were ready and packed, she would arrange for them to be sent to all the houses. The effort to prepare these goodies was tremendous. The love with which it was made was immeasurable.

Her husband also owned a house in the village Kuderu about 50 kilometers from Mysore. Kuderu is a small village in Chamarajanagar district near Mysore. The journey by bus to get to the village was a little over an hour. Rajeshwari would shuttle between Kuderu and Mysore and take all the time and effort to take good care of each of her family members.

The house in the village was a traditional house that had a huge rectangular courtyard in the middle of the main hall. The courtyard was slightly raised from the ground and was open to the sky. A narrow corridor supported by sturdy pillars ran all around the courtyard connecting to the rooms. Rain or shine, one could enjoy the weather by staying indoors through the open courtyard. The toilet and the bathing area were behind the main building and it was a two-minute walk to get there from the main house. Firewood was used for cooking and heating water for baths. The front of the house had a sloping tiled roof to bear the onslaught of the monsoon rains. The house was well-ventilated with sun and fresh air. The mornings were typically welcomed with hymns and the aroma of scented *agarbattis*[31] as offerings to God.

---

[30] *Maagliberu – root locally grown in villages of Karnataka.*
[31] *Agarbattis - incense sticks.*

During the months of March to July, when the mango season set in, the aroma of mangoes from the village farms would fill the house. Big jackfruits also would arrive in plenty from the farms. Cutting the jackfruits was an intensive process. The sticky sap from jackfruit is messy and so a generous amount of oil was applied on the knife and hands before cutting the fruit. Newspapers were spread on the floor to contain the mess. Each fruit bulb which is covered by a fibrous mass had to be removed patiently to extract the fruit. It would take hours to peel, clean and cut the fruit into pieces. But the sweetness of the fruit made all the effort worthwhile. Every summer, when the schools closed, the house was filled with extended families spending their annual break together. It was indeed a cheerful and celebratory ambience.

Festivals were large scale, inclusive celebrations in Rajeshwari's household. The most important ones, such as *Sankranti,* the harvest festival, *Ugadi* celebrating New Year, and *Deepavali,* the festival of lights was celebrated with grandeur. These festivals were celebrated with complete traditions and rituals at her village house. Of all the festivals, the grandest celebration was for the *Gowri Ganesha Puja,* the festival dedicated to Goddess Gowri and her son Lord Ganesha. The celebration involved preparation and serving of food to almost 100 people every day, for two weeks. Rajeshwari had volunteers from her circle of relatives and a few close friends who were as good as family. She planned and organized the entire process from start to end and delegated the tasks to each one as appropriate. There was help at hand with enough efficient people to work, but the key to make it perfect required attention to every detail. It demanded excellent leadership and management skills and Rajeshwari was a master at both!

Year after year, Rajeshwari did all the groundwork for preparation of her homemade snacks and pickles. As Rathna packaged the pickle jars quietly and efficiently, Rajeshwari looked lovingly at her beautiful sister and smiled to herself. But she soon looked back at the tray of dried rice papads that she was filling into containers to store away and heaved a deep sigh. There was one worry that constantly surfaced on her mind. She wondered about Prabhakar. It had been three years since the offer of Rathna's hand in marriage was made to Prabhakar. Unavoidable circumstances on both sides of the family had prevented them from getting engaged or married. When relatives came in occasionally with updates like, "Oh! Prabhakar is now doing MA!" or Did you hear about Prabhakar? He has landed a new job in the city!" Rajeshwari wondered if it was time they moved forward with the wedding.

Prabhakar had moved to Bangalore recently and had got a job as a lecturer in M.E.S college. His uncle had finally sent word that he was coming to talk to Rathna's family about the marriage. Rajeshwari knew that Rathna was working hard to cover the family expenses and she wanted her to settle down soon. Prabhakar had sent his uncle to restart the thread of discussion about the engagement and wedding. Rajeshwari hoped that the talks would go smoothly, and everything would be fine.

The long-awaited day arrived. As per tradition, the elders of the family had to be at the forefront of such talks. Rajeshwari and her husband Venkataramaiah who was also fondly called as KSV greeted Prabhakar's uncle and a variety of snacks were served to the special guests. Rajeshwari had prepared *Upma*, *laddus*, (a sweet snack made of gram flour) and other savories. The talks began after the guests had their fill. It was customary for the bride's side to give money to the groom for the wedding to buy a watch, suit, and shoes and Prabhakar's uncle followed the same. He got straight to the point without any hesitation. "My nephew is now a lecturer, he has a very good job, and holds a high post. He deserves good things," he stated and demanded the wedding be conducted with certain expenses. Rajeshwari and KSV were taken aback. They humbly replied, "But...it is a little too high for us to afford. We will not be able to spend so much. Please understand..." Prabhakar's uncle was not ready to compromise or did not intend to encourage any further discussion on the topic. In a fit of disappointment on the failure of his demand being met, he walked away breaking the engagement. Rajeshwari was heartbroken.

Prabhakar was however unaware of the developments and oblivious to the fact that his own engagement had been called off! News of the broken engagement was slowly spreading and relatives of both the families who had mediated the proposal decided to take the matter seriously into their hands. They intervened to negotiate the demand. Rathna's mother did not want to lose Prabhakar's alliance for Rathna and was ready to pay the negotiated amount. She had seen Prabhakar take on responsibilities of his siblings at a very young age just as Rathna had been doing for her family. She knew that Prabhakar was a good person and a perfect match for Rathna.

By the time, the news of the talks and the developments that followed reached Prabhakar and he hurried to fix the messy situation, it was all sorted. The mediators had successfully intervened on time. Prabhakar was not informed of the details on why the talks had failed, but he learned years later that money was a factor in the talks. He apologized to Rathna for what she and her family were put through. But both Prabhakar and Rathna knew that those days decisions were always taken by the elders and questioning their authority or interfering in their talks was considered disrespectful. However, Prabhakar was a self-made man and this incident remained as a scar on his mind for long. It was probably the last time he sent his uncle to represent him anywhere. He knew that even though his uncle had no wrong intentions and had the best of intentions, his actions were not in accordance with Prabhakar's principles. Money was never an important factor for Prabhakar, more so when it involved sentiments of people. He believed that money and success would follow if one did not deviate from the path of righteousness.

After the broken engagement was fixed, the family was busy with the preparations. Rajeshwari helped conduct the wedding with all the rituals and traditions for her sister. She and her husband had hosted and conducted many weddings and functions for their family members, and this was the wedding of her dearest sister. Her joy and excitement knew no bounds and whatever she did to make her Rathna's special day the best seemed to be nowhere near enough. Such was the love and bond they shared. They were referred to as peas in a pod! Rathna and Rajeshwari were very close to each other and remained so throughout their lives.

Rajeshwari was a gift to the family, especially to her siblings. She was always giving and ever loving. Her husband, KSV, too complemented her personality by being just as generous. Prabhakar admired the couple and revered Rajeshwari from the bottom of his heart. He often wondered, *in today's modern society, relationships have become meaningless. We are becoming more materialistic and selfish. Our minds question and rationalize more, than letting our hearts rule...* and in such a world, Rajeshwari was a blessing to them.

Rajarajeshwari, the name that means queen of queens, was one of the few that ruled the hearts of so many people. Sadly, selfless people like her rarely exist anymore.

Nagarathna

Rathna's alliance was brought to Prabhakar when he was posted as a headmaster in Bekkalale. That was a time when Prabhakar had felt he was settled well in a job and was ready for marriage. When he received a letter from Rathna's brother-in-law seeking Prabhakar's alliance, he was overjoyed. He had seen Rathna earlier and recollected her quiet and mild-mannered nature. She was very beautiful too: slim, fair, with dark, flowy hair. Prabhakar could never have imagined that an alliance of such a perfect girl, who could be highly praised for her beauty and character, would be brought to him. Undoubtedly, he was elated.

Rathna's full name was Nagarathna and she was the fourth of ten children. Rathna had lost her father early in life and just like Prabhakar, had borne the burden of responsibilities of bringing up her siblings. Rathna had grown into a sensitive, charming girl with a pleasing personality that reflected in her strikingly good looks and warm smile. Like any other, Rathna's mother too wanted to see her married and settled well in life. Rathna was already 21 years old and that was well past the average age that most girls in those times got married at. Considering this and the family's situation, her mother's anxiety was expected.

Rathna, however, was not ready for marriage yet. She wanted her younger brother to have a job so that he could take on the responsibilities from her, before she got married. She asked her mother and the other elders of the family for three years' time to help her brother settle down. They were reluctant but decided to convey Rathna' s request to Prabhakar. "Rathna is very happy with the alliance...but...she has asked for three years' time. She wants to see her younger brother settled. So...", her brother-in-law hesitantly informed Prabhakar. He was almost sure that three years was a long wait and Prabhakar may not be ready for it. Prabhakar, though, was relieved to hear of Rathna's decision. It worked well for him as well, since he was still figuring out his career options and a little more time to settle down could only be good for him. "I am ready to wait," he said, much to the joy of Rathna's family.

Prabhakar had seen Rathna at a community ritual gathering. Whenever there is a death in the family of a traditional Brahmin household, a 13-day ritual is performed. It included reading stories from Garuda Purana. Garuda Purana are Hindu scriptures that explain life after death, the significance and meaning of funeral rites as well as reincarnation rites. The sacred book consists of dialogue between Lord Vishnu and Garuda, a kind of bird which is the *vahana* or vehicle of Lord Vishnu. Prabhakar was the designated orator of the Puranas in his village and when such a ritual was held, he would narrate the scriptures to the audience every evening after sunset. Rathna would also come along with her aunt to be part of the audience. She would intently listen to the reading. Prabhakar had seen her at one of these ritualistic reading sessions for the first time. Years later, Prabhakar realized that the decision of having Rathna as his life partner had changed him for the better in his life in many ways. He thanked his lucky stars many a time.

Prabhakar and Rathna were two different people with opposite views and opinions about many things, but this always helped Prabhakar get a better perspective rather than be a cause for conflict. Her sensitivity to relationships and her integrity and principles won Prabhakar over many times. He became more convinced with the passing years that she was an extraordinary woman. He did not fail to recognize the sacrifices she had to make to pull the family through difficult times.

Prabhakar fondly recalls his first day out with his new bride. It was not too long after their wedding. One of his cousins pestered Prabhakar to take his bride out for a movie. He agreed, but the entire family got ready to go with the newlywed couple to watch the movie! Within no time, 15 tickets were booked and all of them set out to the theatre in great excitement. This was the first outing for Prabhakar and his bride. They had to watch the movie sitting in two opposite ends of the row, thanks to their battalion occupying all the seats in between! Prabhakar just got the occasional glances of Rathna across the row. Her simple saree and pleasing smile remain etched in his mind.

In their careers, Prabhakar and Rathna were both very successful. They were admired and respected by many and it was not uncommon to see people line up at their house with some seeking advice, and others, requesting for help. None of them went back empty-handed. They were guided and helped, as appropriate. Everyone who landed in the house was sure to be hosted and welcomed with fresh food and hot coffee. A smile of gratitude lit up every face as they left the house, thanking Prabhakar and Rathna from the depths of their hearts. Prabhakar always admired his wife's ability to run the house efficiently and maintain a good social life, both with equal ease. She would have a full working day but come back and switch easily into her homemaker role and take care of her family without any sign of ever being tired or any complaint of discomfort.

Prabhakar was mostly preoccupied with his work and responsibilities and he would often forget to express his affection to Rathna. One day, just a few years after they were married, Prabhakar decided to surprise Rathna. He set out to shop for a saree and selected one that he thought she would like and would look great on her. He proudly presented it to Rathna with a triumphant smile and waited for her reaction to his first gift. Rathna was indeed very happy and excited as she took it from Prabhakar. Her face lit up as she unwrapped the gift from its cover. But the expression on her face soon changed to disappointment. "Oh my God! What have you bought?", she exclaimed without hesitation. It was a brown saree and looked like an old rag. She realized too soon that her dear husband had no taste. "Well, ok...now tell me, how much did you pay for this saree?", she asked, only to hear something that made her feel worse. "I paid...er...1000 rupees for it", Prabhakar replied, confident that he had made a purchase with a good deal. Rathna nodded her head in disapproval and clarified that the price was in no way justified. "In such times when our pay is meagre and just enough to run our family's expenses, you should not have spent that kind of a huge amount on a saree. It is not right.", Rathna explained. Prabhakar quietly nodded in agreement and thought to himself, "It is just not my thing to understand the tastes of women!"

Prabhakar did not however give up trying other different ways to surprise Rathna and make her happy. One such attempt was on a day that he decided to surprise her after work and took her to a famous South Indian restaurant, 'Krishna Bhavan' which was known for the tasty *dosas*. They took a table and sat down to place their order. Rathna casually looked around and was not happy with what she noticed. Prabhakar realized from her expression that something was amiss, and he looked around too. He did not notice anything wrong. So, he glanced back at Rathna and leaning forward, asked in a low tone, "Rathna, *yenaithu?*" ("What happened?") Is anything wrong?" She nodded her head in disgust, sighed deeply and replied, "Look around you! Did you notice there are only men around here? None of them are with their wives or families. Neither are they carrying food packets back home! How can they do this? Be so selfish? They are all middle-aged men eating and enjoying their food all alone. It is so disturbing to see them not share their happiness with their loved ones...selfish men!" she said the last two words a little too loud. Prabhakar sheepishly looked across the room to see if anyone had been hearing his wife's righteous judgement, while they had assumed that they were only innocently enjoying one tasty meal by themselves. Prabhakar was both amused and felt a sense of pride at the same time. He laughed and shook his head in disbelief but did not dispute her argument. They rose to head out of the restaurant and as they walked out, he whispered to her, "You will be hailed as a 'Woman Savior'!" He chuckled and she smiled back at him.

Prabhakar knew that his wife, with her unique and simple qualities, was a God-given gift. She was independent, modern, religious, and righteous. She had friends from all walks of life and across all religions. Her unbiased faith in all religions and gods were seen in her own home. In her

Puja(prayer) room, she had amulets from her colleagues Pasha, a staunch Muslim, and Komala, a Christian. To her, religion meant faith in a superpower. Be it Allah, Jesus, or Shiva, she would fold her hands and pray in reverence. She always questioned the holy books and literature and passionately argued about spirituality, science, and faith. Prabhakar was always very proud of her and had as much respect for her as love.

Ashwatha

Rathna's family was a big one, with ten siblings in total. Of them, there was Ashwatha, who was Rathna's favorite brother. Rathna cared for him like a typical big sister. She insisted on working and supporting her family until Ashwatha was eligible to be the breadwinner. She had agreed to get married only once he had settled into a good job and could take over her responsibilities.

At the time of Rathna's marriage, three of her older sisters were already wedded and settled into good families. The rest of the siblings - Ammu, Subanni, Ramaa, Shailesh and Mala - were dependent on Ashwatha. They were all either still studying or ready for marriage. The responsibility of getting each of them settled and taking care of the household single-handedly, lay on Ashwatha's shoulders. Despite staring at this uphill task, Ashwatha was a cheerful person. He was full of life and brimming with compassion and kindness. Everyone adored him and was warmed by the presence of his affectionate nature.

Ashwatha was also Rathna's biggest advocate. He never missed a chance to dive into a scene of argument and lend unconditional support to his beloved sister. There was no exception to this rule, not even when the argument was between Rathna and Prabhakar! This act arose from Ashwatha's boundless love for his sister and it often triggered hilarious back and forth conversations between him and Prabhakar. Prabhakar affectionately addressed Ashwatha by the name 'Narada Muni'. 'Narada Muni' in Hindu scriptures is depicted as a Vedic sage who often creates a rift in the heavenly world. These rifts are known to benefit mankind. Ashwatha's interference was similar; mild and unexpected, but ultimately beneficial.

Ashwatha and Prabhakar shared many exclusive experiences and memorable moments. One of them was Prabhakar owing him money that only the two of them knew of. "Hey, you owe me money for the coconuts!" Ashwatha would casually remind Prabhakar at every possible instance. Only they knew the details of this confidential debt, which supposedly dated back to Prabhakar and Rathna's wedding day. It is tradition to give betel leaves, some fruit, and a money coin, as a gesture of gratitude to every guest who attends a wedding in South Indian culture. Ashwatha had decided to give oranges to the guests as it fit his budget better. However, Prabhakar had insisted on coconuts as he felt it would represent a grander gesture than oranges. "But oranges are good enough! Coconuts are too expensive...we should keep our budget in mind", Ashwatha had defended his choice. Prabhakar however convinced him, saying, "Don't worry about that. I will contribute half the amount towards the expense. Let us go with coconuts." Ashwatha had to reluctantly give in to Prabhakar's desire. The money he often reminded Prabhakar of owing him was related to this agreement between them. Rathna was unaware of this negotiation. Ashwatha used it to his advantage at every suitable opportunity he got, and it turned into an amusing topic of banter between the two. "Please pay for my coffee, you owe me for the coconuts!", he would affectionately chide Prabhakar.

Ashwatha and Prabhakar were great friends. Over weekends, when Ashwatha came to Bangalore for his work, he would accompany Prabhakar to run errands together with him. On one such occasion, Ashwatha accompanied Prabhakar to the Cauvery Emporium, the biggest and most well-known showroom for Indian handicrafts in Bangalore. Prabhakar had been assigned a task from his college. He had to select some gifts from the Emporium for visiting dignitaries. The norm was to present them with items made of sandalwood, mostly idols of gods or goddesses. The commonly chosen ones based on general preference was an idol of Goddess *Saraswathi*, the Goddess of learning in Hindu mythology, or of Lord *Ganesha*, the remover of obstacles. Ashwatha and Prabhakar walked around the emporium, admiring a variety of beautiful artistic items. The showroom was filled with a gentle aroma of sandalwood as most of the items were made of it. One need not be a compulsive shopper to give in to the temptation of selecting a piece to take home from the large collection they exhibited. Ashwatha and Prabhakar were not an exception. They felt the urge to buy something and exchanged understanding glances to acknowledge each other's thoughts.

Both their homes were typically adorned with framed pictures or carved idols of gods. Prabhakar's house had a huge, framed picture of Lord Shiva who is the God of Destruction and Goddess Parvathi, wife of Lord Shiva, hung on one plain wall of the main hall. The picture was decorated with a beautiful, garlanded pearl necklace that Rathna had strung. One large clock royally ticked away on the other wall. There were no other decorative pieces and only basic furniture occupied space in the room. They were just enough to cater to the needs and minimum comfort of visitors. This apart, the idea of decorating a house with expensive collectibles was not a way of life. With household expenses looming and the struggle to make ends meet, priorities were clear and adhered to. Expensive artwork or luxurious furniture did not feature in a life beset by mounting school fees, mortgages, loans and providing basic meals for the family.

However, on that visit to the Emporium, the two men succumbed to their desire. Ashwatha could not get his eyes off one big piece: a giant elephant head carved in rosewood. It was very heavy but looked beautiful and was perfectly finished. It was indeed a masterpiece, and anyone would be proud to own it. Prabhakar was hesitant and skeptical about buying such an expensive item but agreed after Ashwatha managed to convince him that it would be treasured for years as a precious buy. They made the purchase, picked up the other gifts and headed home. "See what we got!", Prabhakar exclaimed and excitedly unwrapped the package in a hurry to show Rathna and share their joy with her. Rathna saw the giant elephant head and was bewildered. "This is so big! Where will you hang this in our house?" She shook her head and stared at the men. "This elephant head is fit for a palace and not for the walls of this small house", she concluded.

The piece was bought and there was no option to return it. They had no choice but to hang it on one of the walls. With tremendous effort, a good number of nails were hammered into the designated wall. Once they were set, Prabhakar and Ashwatha hung up their new prized possession. Dusting off their hands, they looked at each other and smiled. They were satisfied with their hard work and the result of it, despite Rathna's opinion. Though it occupied almost half of the wall, they were proud of its majestic look. However, they did not dare argue with Rathna about it! The elephant head hangs elegantly on the wall of Prabhakar's house even today. Whenever Prabhakar looks up at it, he fondly thinks of Ashwatha and reminisces, *"What memorable times Ashwatha and I spent together"*

Unfortunately, Ashwatha was not blessed with a long life. He died of a massive heart attack at a very young age. It was on one of his visits to meet the famous cardiologist, Dr. Cherian in Madras, now called Chennai, that he was told that his heart condition was a serious and life-threatening one. Dr. Cherian had seen Ashwatha's reports after various tests were conducted. He met him in the corridor and asked who the patient was. When Ashwatha answered signaling to himself, Dr. Cherian was astounded. "What! This patient is not supposed to be walking!" He turned around to instruct his support staff. He then asked Ashwatha to join him in the consultation room to discuss his health and further treatment. "Well...it is too risky to touch your heart to perform any surgery. So, you need to take care of your health through medication and proper care", he softly told Ashwatha, patting him gently on his back and leaving him with detailed prescriptions.

Ashwatha had come away from that visit knowing well about his faulty heart and the beating countdown. But he never let his condition bother him or others. In fact, he continued to help everyone as always, to the best of his capacity. However, his heart tired out and gave up one day.

Ashwatha's was a life well-lived; though short in span, it was filled with generosity and compassion till the very end. For Prabhakar, his death was an immense loss and he was inconsolable for a long time after. He had lost his beloved brother-in-law and a very dear friend.

Life in the Garden City

Sriramulu

Prabhakar was blessed with a daughter in the year 1973, a year after their wedding. She was named 'Shri Gowri', after his mother-in-law who had recently passed. In the later years, Prabhakar changed her name to Mamatha as he wanted a modern name for his first born. The name remained her official name ever since. Rathna did not have anyone to help take care of her or the baby. She found it very difficult to handle everything on her own. So, she soon found herself in her sister's house in the village of Kuderu.

While Rathna was at Kuderu, Prabhakar was searching for a house for his entire family: his mother, four siblings, wife, and child. He was looking for a place that would fit his small budget and be able to accommodate all of them.

"That one is vacant, you can take it on rent", Sriramulu said, pointing to the second last house among the row of four houses in the compound. "And that, is the common toilet for all four houses", he added, raising his hand to indicate the far end of the common corridor. Prabhakar nodded and immediately agreed to the rest of the conditions that Sriramulu laid down.

Sriramulu owned this place in Subramanyanagar, which suited all Prabhakar's needs. It was a cow shed which was recently converted into four row homes. He owned multiple cowsheds and had converted one of them to row houses that he could rent out individually. He too lived with his family in the same compound, occupying the main house in the Centre.

Prabhakar and his family moved into their new house. It had one bedroom and a verandah, and they adjusted to the given space comfortably. Prabhakar and Rathna had also considered logistics to their workplaces while they were on the search for a house. This one was perfect in that aspect too. It was close to Prabhakar's college. He could also drop Rathna to the bus stop nearby, from where she could take a direct bus to work.

Sriramulu was a small built man with a thick curly moustache, which was distinctly his unique facial feature. His wife Lalithamma was a friendly and unassuming lady. They had four children. Sriramulu was a well-known personality in the neighborhood. The kids who lived there called him 'Nana', meaning father in Telugu, - a language native to Andhra Pradesh. Sriramulu quite enjoyed the title. He had settled in Subramanyanagar early on and was now one among the oldest residents there. His tenants too were happy with his non-interfering and helpful nature.

It was in this house in 1975, that Gopi, their second child, was born to Prabhakar and Rathna. With their busy work schedules and two children to look after, they were navigating life's struggles. They were however a happy, close-knit, and content family. This beat all the odds and challenges that they were facing in day-to-day life.

"Gopi! No, don't do that!", "Come here, you will hurt yourself, Gopi!" were instructions often heard soon after Gopi had learned to walk and run on his own. There was no stopping this little boy. He had a tremendous amount of energy that seemed inexhaustible! To add to this was his unstoppable mischief. He was extremely naughty, and the entire family had to gather their energy and time to keep a watch on him. He was always on the move, up to one thing or the other. At times, he would chase chickens and hens across the road and at others, jump off walls or low roofs of houses. It was hard to know what his next act would be. One moment he was here and then nowhere near, the next!

It was one bright Sunday afternoon. The kids in the neighborhood were out playing on the street, making the best use of their holiday time. It was a safe street to play on and so, the parents did not worry about monitoring them. In most houses, the parents were busy catching up on weekend chores or getting a bit of much needed relaxation. As evening set, the kids returned to their homes as they were told and always did. But that evening, Gopi did not return.

"Gopi has not come home yet. He must be still on the street or up to some mischief. Can you go and check where this boy is?" Rathna called out to Prabhakar as she was grinding batter for dosas for the coming week. Prabhakar glanced at the clock and looked out to see that it was getting quite dark. He quickly headed out to look for Gopi on the street and then in his usual places of play. He could not find him anywhere. He also rushed through all of Gopi's friends' houses asking each one if they had seen the boy. No one had seen him.

Prabhakar began to panic when he realized there was no sign of Gopi. He knew that he would not have gone too far from the regular where he played. His mind began to race. There had been rumors in the past few weeks about kids being kidnapped! *"What if...our Gopi too...oh God!"* Prabhakar had the worst fears surfacing and he broke into a sweat. He came rushing into the compound of his house. By then, everyone was out of their homes, discussing where Gopi could have gone.

Sriramulu noticed the fear on Prabhakar's face. He gently held his hands and assured him that they would find Gopi soon and everything would be fine. The others too gathered around him and Rathna, who was already in tears by then. "Let us all go in different directions to search for the child", Sriramulu took the lead and dispersed the crowd. He directed groups of people to go on the search and told them where they should look for him. They all began the search, screaming Gopi's name as loud as they could, uttering prayers under their breath. They searched homes, under cots, on the streets, rooftops, and every place they could think of where a child of his age and size would have access to. It was well after midnight and there was no positive news from anyone. The entire family was crying at this point and the neighbors were all awake, sharing their worry and consoling them. Prabhakar held back his tears and tried to remain brave and hopeful. He could not give up and had to be strong for his family. He had recurring thoughts of stories of missing children he had heard of. He fought these thoughts, but they were only coming back stronger. Exhausted, he decided to go to the police station.

Sriramulu too felt it was the right decision to go and register a missing complaint with the police. He said he would accompany him, and they stepped out. Just then he noticed that the lights of the opposite cow shed were still on. He walked over quickly to switch them off before leaving. As he approached the shed and reached out to the switch board, he gasped loudly. He had noticed something on the floor in the corner of the shed. There he was - Gopi!

"Here he is... Prabhakar. Come soon. Look, Gopi is here!", Sriramulu's voice reflected a mix of excitement, relief and shock, all at once. He also lowered his voice after the initial shout out to everyone, to not disturb the child who was sound asleep. Prabhakar, the rest of the family and a few neighbors who were still awake came rushing to the spot. Sriramulu smiled as he pointed to the floor where Gopi had cuddled himself to sleep. Prabhakar stooped down and grabbed the child carefully into his arms, his tears flowing now. He quickly checked if the child was fine and handed him over to Rathna, "See...our child is safe. I knew he would be. God is with us!" Everyone rejoiced and thanked the Almighty for getting the child back and safe. Sriramulu patted Prabhakar on his back and they all returned to their homes after the long and tiring day.

In the quiet of midnight, with only the sound of the crickets to be heard, Prabhakar lay awake in his bed. He recollected the eventful evening and the last scene in the cowshed. Sriramulu had a total of ten cows. Nine of them were sitting down but this one cow was standing in the corner. Under the cow was a small figure of a child in deep, sound sleep. Nobody knew how long the child had been asleep there, but the cow had not sat down for the fear of hurting the child.

Prabhakar knew it was not less than a miracle that the child was unharmed. If the cow had sat on the child, he would not have survived. The mute animal was sensitive enough to know this. She had stood there all the while, silently without moving even a bit. Prabhakar could only associate the incident with the knowledge he had from the scriptures. In the *Vedas*, the oldest of the Hindu scriptures, the cow is associated with *Aditi*, the mother of all the gods. The mother had protected her child that evening. It was with these understanding and tear-filled eyes that Prabhakar and Rathna had folded hands in reverence to the cow before they left the cowshed with Gopi in their arms. Their gratitude to the mother was immense as they looked down at their precious child. Gopi was still asleep, and his face showed all innocence and pleaded 'not guilty' for any of the commotion caused that evening.

Red Scooter

"Gopi is really sick. He has high fever... we should take him to the doctor right now. I am so worried!", Rathna was anxious and teary-eyed as she reported two-year old Gopi's condition to Prabhakar on his return from work that evening. He rushed in to look at Gopi and gently touched his face. He realized why Rathna was so agitated. Gopi was running high temperature and had had convulsions too during the day. Prabhakar glanced at the clock. It was 5:30pm. The nearest available doctor was closed for break time between 4.00 and 6.30 pm. Gopi's convulsions were very worrisome, and they could not risk waiting another hour to consult a doctor. Prabhakar thought of an alternative. He walked as fast as he could, to cross two streets where Dr. Venkatesh lived. He rang the doorbell frantically and as Dr. Venkatesh answered the door, he gathered his breath and said, "I need your scooter.

Please, can I borrow it for a while?" Dr. Venkatesh understood it was an emergency and went inside the house, soon to return with the scooter keys. Handing them to Prabhakar, he quickly asked if any help was needed. As Prabhakar explained, Dr. Venkatesh grabbed the keys back, wore his sandals and he started the scooter and nodded indicating that he was going to ride. Back home, Prabhakar wrapped the child in a blanket and hopped onto the scooter. They went around looking for clinics that were open. It took almost an hour to find one. They arrived at the clinic shortly, and by the time the doctor examined Gopi, his temperature had dropped. The open-air ride on the scooter had reduced his fever. The doctor administered medication and Gopi and Dr. Venkatesh rode back home, relieved.

This incident that happened in 1976, made Prabhakar realize that he needed a vehicle for his family, especially in times of emergency. Prabhakar decided to buy a scooter. So, one fine day, the red scooter with the brand name 'Vijay' from the manufacturer Bajaj, bearing the number plate 3786, arrived at their home.

The scooter was a very heavy one, compared to the models that evolved over the years. The color of the scooter was so unique that it became Prabhakar's identity. People referred to his house as 'Red Scooter House' for many years. Every year, Prabhakar would bring the scooter out for *Ayudha Puja*, a Hindu festival celebrated during *Navaratri[32]*. It is during this time that a veneration of machines, weapons and vehicles is performed. Rathna adorned the red scooter with flowers and an *Aarti[33]* was performed to remove any evil eye and ensure safe

---

[32] *Navaratri - is a Hindu festival that spans nine nights and is celebrated every year in the autumn*
[33] *Aarti - Hindu religious ritual of worship, a part of prayer, in which light is offered in spirit of gratitude*

travels for the family. Over the years, Prabhakar bought other vehicles. But Rathna refused to sell the red scooter as she believed it was a lucky mascot for the family. Though it was not used much later, the scooter would be brought out once a year and cleaned for the *Puja* to be performed, followed by a ride.

"Let us just sell this heavy scooter. We are not even using it and see the space it is occupying!", Prabhakar often complained. Rathna would not listen to any of it. She had only one answer every time the topic of selling the scooter came up between them. "We have so many sentiments attached to this vehicle. It is not just a scooter; it has been part of our family for years now. It has seen all the struggles of our family and been with us through them. And now, you want to sell it?" Rathna would become emotional but she stood firmly by her decision. "I will not let it be discarded and torn apart into spare parts. Never!" The conversation would end there each time and the scooter would probably gleam proudly in its designated corner of the garage.

One day, when Prabhakar was trying to move the scooter, he hurt himself very badly. In that painful moment, he yelled at Rathna saying that he was not going to listen to her anymore. "You know what I will do? I will give this away on a betel leaf. To anyone I feel like!", he declared, indicating with a glance that he was referring to the scooter. His frustration was so high that he had intended to gift the scooter; not even sell it. That was not all. "I will give some change too to spare so that they can take this away from my hands!", he added, clarifying his decision.

The very next day, the family found that the scooter was gone. It had been parked outside all night as Prabhakar had hurt his leg the previous day. Now it was Rathna's turn to vent. She felt so bad that Prabhakar had expressed his anger and frustration at the scooter which held many family memories. Hearing Rathna talk so emotionally about a scooter which was a material thing, Prabhakar felt as if someone from the family had gone missing and not as if something was stolen. Rathna was a very simple person. She loved and respected everyone and everything around her. Be it people, nature, or man-made materials, she cared for them all. Her logic was that when one uses things that bring a sense of comfort and ease in life, one must learn to respect them as well. Her simplicity and explanation would always bring Prabhakar back to his senses. This time was not an exception. Now, he too felt the pain of losing the scooter.

As Prabhakar recalled the nostalgic memories on the red scooter, he was distraught. He envisioned the red scooter being torn apart. The thought hurt him deeply. He decided that he would not allow someone else to dismantle his scooter. After all, how could a thief or stranger have the right to meddle with his prized possession? He immediately headed to the nearest police station. The local Sub Inspector knew Rathna well for she worked in the police department. They recognized Prabhakar as he walked in and quickly offered him a seat. Prabhakar pulled the chair and sat down to report the theft. The police initiated a written report and filed a complaint. "Stolen vehicle, a red scooter", was the brief of the report. An alert was issued to look for the scooter. Five days later, the red scooter was found by two policemen on Tumkur highway, about 50 kms from Bangalore. The vehicle had broken down and the thieves were caught pushing the heavy scooter on the highway. The red scooter finally made its journey back home, elevated gloriously on a tow truck. When it arrived at the police station, Prabhakar was informed to go over and collect it. The red scooter became an object of amusement at the police station where it was parked, eagerly awaiting the owner's arrival. "Sir, even for the theft report of a branded car like Mercedes or Rolls Royce, we have not launched such a wide vehicle hunt! This scooter is indeed privileged. You do not have to sign any papers. You may take this piece of art home", the Sub Inspector laughed and dismissed any further discussion. He went inside, leaving Prabhakar and his red scooter to enjoy their private moment of reunion.

Unmindful of the sight they were to onlookers, Prabhakar smiled, looking lovingly at his long-lost companion. He kick-started the scooter, and in full glory and aplomb, the happy duo headed home. Rathna's joy knew no bounds when she saw Prabhakar and their red scooter around the corner of the road. She had been eagerly waiting with her *Aarti* plate, to discard any evil eye that may have fallen on the scooter from the day it went missing.

Years passed and life brought many changes to Prabhakar and his family. All through, the scooter remained one of their valued assets. It was not a mere vehicle to Prabhakar, but a fond memory of the days when he and his beloved Rathna rode to places on it with their three adorable children.

To this day, the red scooter stands majestically, quietly, in the garage waiting for that one day that it is taken out every year for the festival and the ride. Sometimes seeming to think, *"Maybe, I will earn a place in the museum one day!"*

Landowner

One evening, when Prabhakar came home from work, he noticed that Rathna was crying. He sat down to console her, asking what had happened and why she was so upset. With tears rolling down, Rathna explained, "As planned, we went to meet the lady Speaker of Vidhana Soudha today...". Vidhana Soudha is the seat of the Karnataka State Legislature. Rathna was told by her colleague that the Speaker would help in allocation of land for middle-class families with lower income. She was also informed that those employed in government jobs would be given preference. Rathna and her friend had visited the office to meet the Speaker and request for an allocation of land.

"We waited all day to meet her," Rathna continued to explain, "only to be informed that she had left the office. That is not all. She knew that many of us were waiting to meet her since morning and she just left through the back door without letting us know". Exhausted and tired and the fact that the lady had left in such a manner, not bothering about those who waited in hunger and for long hours, hurt Rathna immensely. As she completed the sad story of the day in between sobs, Prabhakar realized that she had expressed her intention of owning a house. It dawned upon him that his wife was trying to get them to live under a roof they could call their own, however small. He knew that he had to do something as well.

The following day, Prabhakar met his uncle, Jayasheela Rao, to discuss the matter with him. To his luck, his uncle was to meet the chairman of BDA, (Bangalore District) office soon and said that he would put in a word as well. BDA is a government agency responsible for zoning and allocation of land. Jayasheela Rao arranged for Prabhakar to meet the chairman personally and put forth his request. When Prabhakar met him, the chairman realized that his children went to the same college where Prabhakar was teaching. In fact, Prabhakar was their teacher. The Chairman said "Meshtre, consider it done". A land was allocated to Prabhakar in the west of Bangalore, in an area called 'Judges Colony'. Prabhakar was very happy with the quick allocation and the area too. However, he soon realized that they did not have enough funds to pay immediately for the land. Both Rathna and Prabhakar applied for a two month extension period, stating that they would need some time to raise the amount. The request for extension was accepted.

After a long period of wait and efforts to gather funds, along with sanction of a loan, Prabhakar and Rathna bought the piece of land. The land was registered in their name and this was the first step in realizing their dream of owning a home. They were ecstatic. Even though there was a big sewage drain running in front of the land, it did not dampen their joy. They knew that getting this piece of land was a big effort and it would have cost a lot more if it was in any other location. They would not have been able to afford any more than what they had. They were genuinely content with their purchase.

The next step in the process was to get a plan sanctioned for the house and begin the construction. Prabhakar met his cousin Anantha to proceed with this and with the help of more loans, he began the work. Prabhakar trusted Anantha completely and handed over total responsibility of the construction to him. He was naive and did not realize that he was being cheated. He was shocked to eventually find out that the workers were not being paid on time, though he used to regularly give money to Anantha as per the expenses stated by him. The workers had stopped coming in to work and when about half the house was completed, the construction came to a halt. Prabhakar did not know what to do. He went to visit Anantha and requested him, "Please sort this soon and restart the work, Anantha. Rathna and I have invested a lot in this house, and it needs to be completed as soon as possible." For the next few months, Prabhakar had to ride every day for about 50 kilometers to meet him and persuade him to finish the construction. There was absolutely no effort from Anantha's side, whatsoever. One fine day, Anantha declared bankruptcy. "What? How could you do this? I trusted you completely and now you are just washing your hands off! This is unfair, Anantha...", Prabhakar said shaking his head in disbelief of what he had heard. To make things clear, Anantha simply handed Prabhakar a bankruptcy paper and dismissed him without further explanation. Dejected and pained by being cheated by someone he had trusted blindly, Prabhakar returned. He applied for another bank loan and as soon as it was sanctioned, he requested the workers to come back to work. He assured them saying, "Here are your dues. Please continue the work, starting tomorrow. I promise, hereafter all of you will get paid on time. Focus on the work and complete it soon." Then on, he personally visited the site every day to ensure that the house was completed as planned.

Nothing came easy in life for Prabhakar. Every step was a struggle and his path were laid with obstacles and challenges. Yet, he never complained. Nor did he ever resign himself to fate. He did not know where he got this positive outlook to life, but it was his biggest asset. He was always grateful for it.

The house was complete, and the house-warming ceremony was conducted in a simple manner. Prabhakar and Rathna invited their close family and friends to share in their joy and grace the occasion. Prabhakar named the house 'Jayasheela', a fitting dedication to his dear uncle who had guided and unconditionally helped him at every crossroads of his life. The house was a dream fulfilled and became a haven of love, warmth, and care for Prabhakar and his family.

Landlord

After the housewarming ceremony of 'Jayasheelaa', Prabhakar decided to give the house on rent, to help him repay the loans availed. He passed a word around and soon, a person named Shetty, who hailed from Mangalore, approached Prabhakar and expressed his interest in taking the house on rent. Shetty mentioned that he was a businessman and owned small industries in the outskirts of Bangalore. He appeared decent and was well-mannered. Prabhakar approved of him and put forth details of the rental agreement. "You will need to pay a deposit of Rs. 300 and a rent of Rs. 100 every month." Shetty agreed to the terms and moved in with his family soon after.

The following month, Prabhakar went to meet Shetty and collect the rent for the first period of occupancy. Shetty warmly welcomed him, offering a cup of tea. After they exchanged greetings and enquired about each other's wellbeing, Prabhakar brought up the topic of payment of rent. Shetty lowered his head and after a brief pause, explained, "How do I say this to you...? All my payments are stuck with a vendor. He has promised to clear them soon. I will definitely pay the rent next month. Please understand." Prabhakar could relate all too well with the struggles of a middle-class family man. He agreed to meet Shetty the next month and left.

Prabhakar went again after a month, with hopes of collecting the rent for two months. He too needed money but had compromised on humanitarian grounds. He was dejected to receive the same response again from Shetty. This routine went on for a long time until Prabhakar lost his patience. When he went to meet Shetty after 10 months, Prabhakar decided to give him an ultimatum. When he walked in through the gate, he found the house in darkness. He looked around the neighborhood and found that all other houses had power supply except for this one. Prabhakar enquired about the power supply when Shetty answered the door. He casually replied that he had been out of the city on work and the electricity board had cut the supply in his absence. He did not follow it up with any explanation. Without saying a word, Prabhakar went to the Electricity Board office the next day to enquire about the supply to his house. To his utter dismay, he found out that the electricity bill had not been paid for 10 months! It was a moment of realization for him that Shetty had not only defaulted on paying the rent, but also from paying for any of the utilities. He had been doing this for 10 months, ever since he occupied the house.

Prabhakar was confused and did not know how to confront Shetty. He returned home, exhausted, and shared his woes with his current landlord, Sriramulu. Sriramulu heard the story and was angry beyond words. He asked Prabhakar to hop on to his scooter immediately. Prabhakar did not know what his intention was but got his friend Professor Ranganath along, and the trio strode together on their mission to evict Shetty. Sriramulu was a small man whereas Shetty was tall and big of build. As the three of them rode towards their destination, Prabhakar wondered if the intimidation was going to work! He had no idea of what was to come but knew that they were going to sort this out together.

On meeting Shetty, Sriramulu sprang into action even before anyone could speak. It seemed as though he was waiting for the moment and was fully prepared to confront him! He jumped up to Shetty, held his collar with one hand and pointed an index finger at him, speaking in an aggressive tone. "You have not paid this teacher rent for so many months! You have troubled him enough! Now, we want you to leave quietly or else...." Shetty was taken aback by the sudden outburst. He felt insulted and was angry at the way the three men had barged in to attack him. He looked at the three of them and pointed to Prof. Ranganath who was the quietest person in the room. "I will talk only to him", he declared as if he had been given a choice. Sriramulu would hear no more of anything that Shetty had to talk or explain. He walked closer to Shetty, looked him straight in the eye and said, "No more talk! There will only be action next time. Leave, or be ready to face it!" Prabhakar was a silent onlooker through the entire episode and he wondered what Sriramulu meant as he left Shetty with these threatening words. As they all stood in silence, Shetty walked out in a rage, started his scooter, climbed onto it and rode away.

Prabhakar and Prof. Ranganath were short of words after the intense scene. They felt that the ambience had heated up with the argument and no more talk was required at the moment. They also left soon after. As they rode back home,

Prabhakar wondered how this was all going to unfold. "*Will Shetty vacate the house under pressure, or will he create more trouble?*" he thought anxiously, but there was nothing he could do right then. Only wait and watch.

The next morning, Prabhakar received a call from the police station asking him to go and meet the police inspector. He knew that Shetty was up to something after the incident of the previous day. He was right. A complaint had been filed against him for taking people along to threaten Shetty and force him to vacate the house. Prabhakar explained the situation and his helpless position to the police inspector. He also mentioned that his wife, Rathna, worked in the police department. The inspector was alert when he heard Rathna's name. The comradery that police force and military share in every country is known to everyone. They do not bear any injustice done to their fellow officers. The police inspector immediately called Shetty. He accused him of doing wrong by not paying the rent on time for so long. "It could be a case against you, for cheating and swindling innocent people. Are you aware of it?" he warned him. "Pay all the rental dues right away and I do not want any excuse from you!" The inspector finished his statement on a loud note and left Shetty with no chance to talk further. Prabhakar was relieved with the warning issued by the inspector. With a formal action from the police, he was hopeful that this would resolve his problems with Shetty and, his endless visits to the house to plead for payment.

When Prabhakar went the next day, he found it was not locked and there was no sign of anyone. As he further went in, he realized that the house was empty. Shetty had escaped without paying him a single rupee for all the 10 months that he had occupied the house! Prabhakar was shocked and very disappointed about being cheated this way. He then decided not to rent out the house anymore. He was mentally exhausted and could not deal with another situation like this one.

On returning home, Prabhakar poured out his woes and the painful story of Shetty's escape to Rathna. He also discussed his next plan of themselves occupying the house. She readily agreed. To them, peace of mind was more important than anything else. They knew that they would be able to face financial struggles somehow, like they always had. It was also a happy decision for them to be able to live in the house that they had built with so much effort and care. Finally, 'Jayasheela' was occupied by the rightful owners.

Dodd Mori Kathe: Story of the sewage pit

After the family moved into 'Jayasheela', they began to slowly adjust to the new area, neighbors, and surroundings. When Prabhakar and Rathna had purchased the land, they were oblivious to the long sewage pit running along the entire stretch of the road. They were very excited to be allotted the land and the fact that they would soon have a house they could call their own had overtaken every other aspect. Only when they started living in the house did they realize the limitations they would face due to the infamous *Dodd mori*[34], the big sewage pit. The kids who belonged to the houses on this street could not play on the road for the fear of falling into the pit. So was the case with Prabhakar and Rathna's children. It was deep underground but was an exposed sewage canal running along the front of all the houses. The smell too was sometimes intolerable and despite numerous efforts from the residents to

---

[34] *Dodd Mori - meaning a big sewage pit in Kannada language*

get the attention of the government to investigate the issue, all they got was a wall constructed around the pit. It was, however, still exposed and one could hear the constant flow of sewage water.

One evening, Prabhakar was riding down the road on his red scooter and he saw a group of people in front of his house staring down the sewage pit. His heart skipped a beat and then sank in fear. The first thought that rushed into his mind was that what if one of his kids had accidently fallen into the *Dodd mori!* His heart raced as he hurriedly parked his scooter and ran towards the crowd that was still talking in whispers and intently looking down the drain. As he got closer, he could hear a long *moo.* He peeped in and saw that a calf had fallen in and was crying out for help. The calf had accidentally fallen while grazing. Folks explained to Prabhakar, "Sir, this sewage drain runs deep in portions but the end of the drain is on upper ground and is shallow so the calf can be rescued only if we can lure the calf to walk a few kms to the shallow end." Prabhakar realized that this meant that they had to chase the calf inside the pit to guide it to rescue. It was getting dark and the calf was too scared to move. Prabhakar joined in the rescue efforts. He requested the folks to stop screaming and shouting since the calf was too scared and too confused and was not moving. They had to come up with other options. Finally, they requested for a volunteer whom they tied in ropes and lowered him to the frightened animal. The volunteer then fastened ropes to the frightened animal so that it could be lifted. There were loud claps and celebrations when the calf was rescued. That day's rescue mission was accomplished, but in Prabhakar's mind, his mission had just begun.

With this incident, Prabhakar realized that the sewage was nothing less than a safety hazard and something had to be done about it. He wrote petitions to the government demanding immediate action from the concerned department. He did not leave any stone unturned. He started a signature campaign and wrote articles in daily newspapers to draw attention.

The second significant incident occurred on a summer night. The windows of the house were kept open at night for ventilation. Prabhakar and Rathna had just retired for the night after a long, tiring day, and were fast asleep. Rathna was woken up from deep sleep by something she felt around her neck. It was a human hand! She sprung up from her bed and screamed and shook Prabhakar awake. Prabhakar woke up with a jolt and immediately grabbed the hand that was just about to pull itself out through the window. Before he could switch on the light, the thief broke his hand free and ran away dropping a flashlight. Prabhakar shouted out loud, "*Kalla Kalla*...thief, thief!" The neighbors woke up and switched on the lights in their houses. They rushed to Prabhakar's house and frantically started looking for the thief. Chain-snatchers at night on the prowl to snatch chains through open windows of houses was a common crime at that time. The search party was now spread across the road, wondering aloud, "Where did he go? He could not have run far so soon...must be somewhere close. Come on, let us search!" Just then, it occurred to Prabhakar that he had not investigated the sewage pit, right outside his home. He flashed the light into the pit and behold! There he was the chain thief! He called out to the others, "Come, look. He is here. We got him!" People swarmed to the spot where Prabhakar was standing, looking down into the *mori*. They screamed at the thief in chorus, ordering him to come up. But the thief promptly refused. They had to keep an eye on him until dawn till one of the neighbors could go and get the police. Finally, the thief was pulled up from the pit with a rope and taken away into police custody.

This incident made Prabhakar even more determined. He stepped up his plea to the government through the media. He added all the supporting stories: about the thief, the calf and how even the kids could not play on the road due to this problem. He made sure to repeatedly write articles every week to make his petition stronger. Finally, the authorities noticed that they were constantly in the limelight that Prabhakar was shining on them. They had to put an end to it and so they sent workers to close the sewage drain immediately. Prabhakar stood to monitor the work while it was getting done to ensure that it was properly executed. As the work was progressing, the workers complained that there were not enough iron pillars to finish the job. Prabhakar diligently followed up with the suppliers so that the job would be finished without delay. The day the work was completed was a day of celebration in the neighborhood. Neighbors hailed Prabhakar as their hero. They came to meet and personally thank him. They applauded him on his sense of civic duty as a sincere citizen. Thanks to Prabhakar, *Dodd mori kathe* was finally a 'closed' chapter.

Solar eclipse and the baby

When Prabhakar became a father to his firstborn, Mamatha, he was hesitant to hold the baby. He was overwhelmed by her tiny feet and little fingers and feared that his rough hands may hurt her delicate, rosy skin. Soon after, they had a second child, a boy, who was named 'Gopi', nicknamed after his dad Gopalaswamaiah. Rathna often teased Prabhakar saying, "You are a father of two kids now. Still, you are afraid of carrying and cuddling them. All you do is play with them by rattling keys or ruffling their hair!" Prabhakar knew she was right and would look at her with a sheepish grin while she laughed out loud.

Prabhakar decided to prove himself to Rathna and show that he was as comfortable with kids as anyone else. So, one day, he picked Gopi up and placed him on his shoulders and started dancing around in the room. Gopi who was then a one-year-old, noticed an open socket on the ceiling and was attracted to it. He reached out and put a finger in! This sent a huge shock through the child and Prabhakar. Both father and child were thrown to the floor within seconds. They looked at each other and after a moment of 'shock', they burst into giggles. Hearing the laughter, Rathna came into the room. She was amused to find the duo on the floor, still laughing. "What happened? How did you both fall?", Rathna asked. Prabhakar told her what had happened and how they had landed on the floor. "So much for this 'electric bonding'!" sighed Rathna, fondly looking at the father and son duo.

When Rathna was seven months pregnant with their third child, there was a total solar eclipse in Bangalore. Solar eclipses in Hindu religion are inauspicious and many things are prohibited around the time of the eclipse. One of them concerns pregnant women, who are not allowed to go outside the house during the time the phenomenon occurs. They are asked to stay inside a room, with minimum exposure to the sun. Prabhakar, however, did not believe in any of this and dismissed it as a mere superstition. He was keen on showing Rathna the eclipse. He made an elaborate arrangement of mirrors that would reflect the sun's shadow on the wall inside the living room of the house. As the solar eclipse passed, when it was the crescent phase of the sun, Prabhakar called out to Rathna. "Come! Look at the reflection of the sun on the wall. Step out just for a second, you can see it!" He was excited and wanted to share the moment with his dear wife. The elders in the house chided him for it. Prabhakar ignored them all and insisted. Rathna hesitated but seeing her husband's excitement and not intending to disappoint him, she came out to see the reflection. She stayed out for less than a minute.

Two months later, Rathna went into labor. Prabhakar rushed her to the hospital and waited eagerly outside the labor ward. As he was pacing up and down in anxiety, the nurse came out of the room, holding a little bundle. "It is a girl", the nurse announced, smiling at Prabhakar. He smiled and extended his hand to take the newborn into his arms. As he held the little one, he noticed something. She had a big mole on her forehead near the left eyebrow. It was shaped exactly like the solar eclipse that he had shown Rathna a couple of months ago! Prabhakar could not believe his eyes. He handed the child back carefully to the nurse and walked to the hospital canteen to get himself a cup of coffee. As he sipped the coffee, he wondered what he would tell his wife. *"Was her superstition true? Were all the elders right about what they said?"* Prabhakar knew that there was no science to prove that exposure to eclipses during pregnancy could cause birth marks in the child. He had studied that one should simply not look at the sun directly during eclipse because the rays are harmful to the retina. *"Was I wrong?"*

Poring through these thoughts, he finished his coffee, paid for it, and mindlessly put the change back into his shirt pocket. He walked back to the room, still lost in his own analysis of science and faith. Just then, the nurse had cleaned the baby and came in to hand her over in a wrapped bundle, to the mother. He looked on curiously to see Rathna's reaction to the baby and her mole. As he glanced down at the baby in the nurse's arms, he noticed that the baby did not have a mole! *"How can a mole disappear?!"* He immediately looked at the nurse and notified her. "I am sure that the baby shown to me immediately after the delivery had a black mole, right here...", he said pointing to his left eyebrow. "It was...well...shaped like a crescent sun on the baby's forehead. This baby has somehow been exchanged with ours!" The nurse was taken aback by how Prabhakar was so sure. She and the other staff looked at him as he spoke about the mole without any ambiguity. Rathna was listening too, though she did not fully understand what was going on. Soon, there was commotion in the ward.

The nurse went back to the nursery to check. She returned in some time, with another baby in her arms. She was nervous. "I am sorry. Very sorry, there was a slight confusion and the babies got exchanged", she profusely apologized and acknowledged her mistake. She handed over the baby that she had brought to Prabhakar. He nodded to the nurse accepting her apology and bent over to show the baby to Rathna. He pointed to the mole, saying, "See, this girl is so lucky. She saved us from getting someone else's baby!"

The girl was named 'Pannaga' and was forever teased by the family as the 'exchanged baby'. Superstition or otherwise, Prabhakar was grateful for the mole that got their precious baby girl back to where she rightly belonged - in their loving arms.

God v/s Prabhakar

Prabhakar was not a very religious person. But he followed all rituals and *pujas*[35] diligently for the sake of Rathna. He believed that a person attains his goals only through hard work and determination and not by merely relying on God. Rathna, on the other hand, was extremely religious. She believed that faith in God and deep reverence could move

---

[35] *Pujas – prayers in Kannada*

mountains that lay as obstacles on a person's path in life. There were several incidents in their life too that Rathna strongly believed to be signs from God to make Prabhakar see the light. She would chide him when such things happened because she believed that it was God who guided him in the right direction. Prabhakar, however, brushed aside all of it as mere coincidence.

Nanjangud temple, near Mysore, was the abode of their family deity. This ancient temple is very famous and attracts thousands of devotees everyday who come to offer their prayers to the main deity of Lord Shiva, also called Nanjundeshwara. On one such visit, Rathna was standing in a queue saying her prayers in silence, as she waited for her turn to offer *vasthra*[36], a piece of silk cloth as an offering to Lord Ganesha. In mythology, Lord Ganesha is the son of Lord Shiva. He is the deity with an elephant head and is accompanied by a mouse called *Mooshaka* as his vehicle. The belief is that Lord Ganesha can remove any obstacles from the world with the help of *Mooshaka* who can slither through narrow pathways, even in the darkness of the night. Clothes, jaggery, coconuts, fruits and flowers are the common offerings that devotees make to this Lord. As the queue was long and moving very slowly, Prabhakar began to lose his patience. He paced up and down. They had spent all morning doing the temple rounds and offering elaborate prayers to each deity. They had to leave by the afternoon bus to Mysore and it was getting late. He finally lost his patience and shouted at Rathna for causing delay. He gently pulled her aside from the queue and whispered, "Your Lord has so much! Why would he need the two-piece cloth that you are giving him?!" Rathna tried to reason with him, "It is not like that. You know we..." But Prabhakar cut her short. He would not listen to a word from her. "Enough of it. We have prayed

---

[36] *Vastra – a piece of cloth in Kannada*

enough. It is getting too late now. Come...", he interrupted and got her out of the queue. He walked straight towards the bus, with Rathna tagging along. As they reached the bus, she turned around to face the temple and joined her hands. She bowed and said a quick prayer asking for forgiveness from the Lord on behalf of her husband and reluctantly boarded the bus.

A few days later, one afternoon, Prabhakar was in the middle of a lecture at college. The class was about the poems of Kabir, the famous Sufi poet. As he was reciting the *Doha*[37] and was immersed in explaining the deeper meaning of it, he felt a tickle inside his pants. He ignored it at first and went on with his lecture. He suddenly felt something creep stealthily into his pants. He was startled and let out a gasp. He looked up from his book to face the class. All eyes were on him waiting for the *Doha* to be explained. Prabhakar could not bear to stand still anymore. He made an excuse and dashed to the restroom. As he removed his clothing, he was in for a big surprise from a small creature. It was a little mouse! The mouse ran out of his pants, equally surprised by its sudden exposure, and scuttled away. Prabhakar wondered how the little thing had found its way into his pants. He had no idea. He sighed and with a sense of relief, quickly returned to his class that was attentively waiting to hear the rest of Kabir.

That evening when he got home, he narrated the incident to Rathna. Her eyes widened as Prabhakar looked on. He knew that her mind was trying to seek an explanation for the incident. He was right, she did have one! She swiftly raised her right hand and pointed behind her right shoulder, signaling to the past. She recalled the incident at the Nanjangud temple, where Prabhakar had not let her offer clothes to her Lord. She declared with utmost certainty, "It was Lord Ganesha who sent

---

[37] *Doha - couplet*

his agent, Mooshaka, the little mouse to teach you a lesson!" She burst out laughing as she completed her story, "You were stripped off your clothes because you did not offer him the two-piece cloth!"

Prabhakar was both shocked and amused at her interpretation. He nodded his head and joined Rathna in her laughter, agreeing to this probability. He also knew what he would be expected to do to mend his mistake. He had to pay a hefty "fine" for the impatience he had shown at the temple. Rathna made him withdraw his savings from the bank and got a silver *vasthra* made. They offered it to Lord Ganesha on their next visit to Nanjangud. Rathna was at peace knowing well that her Lord was now pleased.

To Prabhakar, religion meant duty. He respected religion but gave more importance to one fulfilling his/her duties. However, he did not question Rathna even once about her undeterred surrender to God. In fact, he sometimes wished that he too had that kind of resolute faith in the Almighty. The two of them adopted religion differently. He regularly chanted *Shlokas*[38] but Rathna did much more. She was a devout woman and followed all rituals and fasting without any deviation. Prabhakar supported her in all her religious tasks. He respected her wishes and took her to temples and shrines that she wanted to visit. Prabhakar had no idea about most of the deities and their significance. Nevertheless, he followed Rathna earnestly on her rounds in temples and just did whatever she did. Sometimes, blindly.

On one of their visits to Ghati Subramanya, a temple near the outskirts of Bangalore, Prabhakar was following Rathna as she went about her prayers. He folded his hands and

---

[38] *Shlokas - religious hymns*

started to pray. Little did he realize that he was facing a building that displayed a board reading, *Sundasge Dhari* meaning "Way to the toilet"! Rathna noticed this and nudged him on his shoulder, laughing. Prabhakar opened his eyes to see that he was praying to a toilet building! He sheepishly broke into laughter and said "After I married you, look what I am praying to! Toilet buildings!!" and the two of them could not stop giggling.

Rukmini

Bangalore, 1982. After his marriage to Rathna, Prabhakar had moved to Bangalore with a big family consisting of his siblings and a few relatives. With so many commitments towards his siblings, Prabhakar could barely do anything exclusively for Rathna. They both were focused on taking care of the family and all their needs. Their sole aim was to get each of the siblings settled in their lives and this called for innumerable sacrifices on their behalf. But Prabhakar and Rathna worked tirelessly, together as a team.

Rukmini, Prabhakar's sister who was fondly called 'Rukku', had come of age and had to be married off. After a few years of saving money for the wedding, they found a suitable alliance for her and the wedding day was set. All arrangements had been made with attention to every small detail. The big day arrived. As was customary, the groom and the wedding party were welcomed on the first day. The chefs had accounted for approximately 100 guests and had prepared batter accordingly for steamed *idlis* to be served as a light meal for the groom's party. But only 25 guests arrived! The chef was devastated. So much of the batter would go to waste. "We have used only a quarter of the batter! There is so much left over. We will have to make use of it somehow...else it will be fermented and wasted. Let me think of making an improvised dish out of this. Maybe with some spices and other add-ons...", the chef lamented to his assistant cook, letting his mind get creative in salvaging the batter.

The next morning, an aroma of spiced *idlis* filled the air of the marriage hall. The guests started to make their way hurriedly to the dining hall. The appetizing aroma made their stomachs roar with hunger pangs. Their faces lit up as the special item was served alongside other breakfast dishes of *Pongal*[39] and *Dumroot Halwa*[40]. The guests devoured the spiced *idlis*, uttering words of praise for it and shaking their heads in undisputed approval. Within no time, the special *idlis* vanished! All of it had made their way to feed the first batch of guests. As the other relatives made their way to the dining hall and were seated for their meal, there was no sign of the spiced idlis. Only *Pongal* and *Dumroot Halwa* were served. Now, the hungry guests were also angry. They felt that only 'special' invitees got the 'special item' and the rest were treated differently with a serving of normal breakfast dishes. As the word spread, there was commotion in the hall and faces with signs of obvious disappointment were seen all around. Prabhakar noticed this and started to feel tense. Once again, he felt that familiar rush of fear and the worst thoughts that come with it. He made his way to the kitchen to discuss with the chef. As he walked, his steps and head felt heavy, he thought *"What do I do now? Marriages have been cancelled for the slightest of mistakes and*

---

[39] *Pongal - a steam-cooked dish made of lentils and rice seasoned with pepper*
[40] *Dumroot Halwa - a pumpkin dessert.*

silly reasons...and this is an important matter - a matter of food!"
In fact, the most important part of a wedding is food. It is a measure of hospitality extended to the groom and his relatives. Prabhakar knew this and was obviously worried about what had happened.

Prabhakar rushed into the kitchen and directly instructed the chef to make more of the special *idlis*. The chef stared blankly at Prabhakar and threw his hands up in a helpless gesture. "I don't even remember what I mixed in the batter. I was just thinking of how not to waste the leftover batter and...and just got creative with some of the ingredients which were available on the shelves. Now, the batter is all done, and I cannot even recollect what I added!", he confessed. Prabhakar felt lost. His fearful thoughts returned. "How can I even say that it was an item of the chef's improvement to the previous day's batter? That will make things worse!". The groom's uncle was furious and demanded an explanation from the chef. The chef did not utter a word and he got busy with cooking the next big meal which was the afternoon lunch and there were at least 25 items on the menu to be cooked. A lot of chaos and discussion followed before a mediator could finally calm the situation down. For a long time to come, only Prabhakar and the chef knew the actual story behind the special *idlis*. To this day, Prabhakar feels amused at how folks preferred improvised leftover food over fresh food.

Despite the initial hiccup, the wedding went off smoothly and all the rituals were completed. Prabhakar was relieved once the day was over and as he pulled a chair to rest for a while, he looked at his wife lovingly and smiled to himself. Rathna had worn a simple saree with a not-so-noticeable small tear in her blouse that could not be fixed in time. She had not bothered much about her appearance and chose to be simple. She had given her best sarees to Rukmini and decked her up with her own wedding jewelry. Prabhakar thanked his lucky stars yet again to be blessed with a life partner like Rathna. In the years to come, her many sacrifices paved the way for the family to cross adversities and make a better life. Her devotion and love for her family were unconditional and boundless.

Tiger Prabhakar

One morning, as Prabhakar parked his red scooter in its designated space outside college and started walking towards the entrance, he noticed a group of people down the road. 'Kishore Kendra, an elementary and high school that belonged to the MES group of institutions that was located down the road from the college. As he walked closer to the group of people, he noticed that a man with a white cap on his head was at the center of the group and was surrounded by school kids. Prabhakar smelt something fishy and quickened his pace towards them. He saw that the man was handing packets to the kids and talking in whispers. He was sure that some suspicious activity was going on within the group. He immediately confronted them and demanded an explanation from the man, "Hey! What is happening here? Who are you and what are you selling? Show me!" The man was startled as he heard Prabhakar's authoritative voice. He looked up to face Prabhakar and realized that he was caught and had been cornered. The kids too were frightened by Prabhakar's intervention and quickly dispersed. The man pushed Prabhakar aside and made his way through to run as fast as he could. Prabhakar's instincts kicked in. He chased the man and got hold of his bag. He grabbed the bag, but the man managed to escape from his hold and ran away. Prabhakar moved to one side of the road, gathered his breath, and opened the bag. He was shocked! There were several small white packets inside the bag, and he recognized that they were drugs! He went up to the security in college and informed him about the incident. They reached out to the local police station for help to get rid of the drugs.

The following day, when Prabhakar finished his classes and came out of college, he found that his scooter was smashed. He was aghast. *Who could have done this?* The college security and the police had warned him the previous day that he might be a victim to the drug gang's anger and revenge. After all, Prabhakar's act had resulted in a huge loss for them. They had seen Prabhakar and it was easy for them to reach him. People asked him to stay home till the situation cooled down a little. Prabhakar refused, saying "I have only done my duty and I feel proud about it. No one can harm me in any way. Let them continue to threaten me...I am not afraid." Over the next few days, as he had expected, members of the gang tried different ways to scare him. They continued to damage his scooter and trouble him indirectly. Prabhakar ignored all of it and eventually the troublemakers gave up and stopped their heinous acts. Prabhakar was hailed and appreciated by parents and the college management for his timely and heroic act. He had done his foremost duty as a true educator and guardian of the students. He had broken a very dangerous chain which would have otherwise damaged the lives of young students. He had busted a drug racket! After this incident, he was bestowed the title of 'Tiger Prabhakar', a name borrowed from a famous movie star who played roles of a cop who busted criminals in *Kannada* movies. To this day, some of his old students affectionately and proudly refer to him by the name – Tiger Prabhakar.

MPL Sastry

Professor MPL Sastry was one of the founders of M.E.S College. The reputed institution had had a humble beginning with only a handful of students and teachers. Today, it stands among the top few on the list of prominent colleges in the country. Value-based education at an affordable cost is the motto of the college and to this day, M.E.S. is ranked the best in high quality of education.

Prof. Sastry was an epitome of discipline and values. His principles of education reflected in his untiring work toward building a college of high reputation and caliber. In today's times, education has become a mere business and a commodity rather than a reverent duty. Institutions like M.E.S are rare indeed that have adhered to their founding mission, following the dreams of its founders.

Prabhakar was deeply influenced by Prof. Sastry. He had inspired him in many ways through the years of his career. He recollects how Sastry used to walk through the hallways while classes were going on. He would look through his black-rimmed glasses, and had a quiet, but certain way of making his presence known. He would open a couple of closed windows, close a few other open ones, and randomly check attendance registers. He regularly made his rounds to ensure that everything was running smoothly. He would greet one and all who crossed his path but strangely, never seemed to smile at anyone. This was known to all, but none knew the reason. One day, Prabhakar decided to take the liberty of asking him about this. "Sir, I have a question. In fact, many of us have the same question. You greet us all with warmth and regard, but why is it that you never smile, sir?" MPL Sastry was taken by surprise at the sudden and straight question from Prabhakar. He paused for a few seconds and quipped, "I was so busy building an institution for generations to come. I did not think of laughing or smiling. The habit must have stayed with me through the years." Prabhakar nodded and folded his hands in respect at the greatness of the man. He thought about the effort and sacrifice that stalwarts of educational institutions had to make, so that many generations to come would get the right education. Every teacher had a sense of ownership and accountability towards the students and the institution. An educator's job was one of the noblest of professions; one that molded the youth, the community, and indeed, the nation.

Professor Sastry was deeply involved with all the activities of the college, including finances. He kept a keen eye on income and expenditure and was always cognizant about frivolous spending. He believed that money should be neither earned unjustly nor be spent without its assured worth in return.

Prabhakar recalls an incident that occurred one monsoon season. As he stepped out of college to return home one evening, the dark clouds had gathered bringing a sign of torrential downpour. He shook his umbrella to spring it open but realized it was broken. He needed a new one immediately. He hurriedly stepped out of the college to a nearby store and bought a fine-looking umbrella for 150 rupees. He was convinced that it was a good price and did not think of negotiating with the shopkeeper. He flaunted his new buy and walked with perceptible pride. Professor Sastry passed by him and noticed the new umbrella. He stopped and asked Prabhakar, "That is a nice umbrella. Is it new? How much did you pay for it?" Prabhakar was not ready for this question. He knew Professor Sastry too well. He was a good negotiator and always got good bargains for anything that was purchased for the college. Prabhakar thought for a moment. *Even though the umbrella is for my personal use, he will believe I unnecessarily paid more! He will not be impressed with my ability if I tell him the correct price.* "Sir, I got this umbrella from Bombay (now 'Mumbai') and that too at a very good wholesale price. It was only 50 rupees!" he grinned, happy with his presence of mind and quick response.

Professor Sastry was indeed impressed! He nodded his head, as a sign of appreciation. "Very good price! Can you get one for me?" he asked. "Sure sir, why not!", came Prabhakar's unhesitant reply. *Not a big deal,* he thought and smiled to himself. After a few days, he went back to the same shop and bought another umbrella for 150 rupees. He headed to Professor Sastry's house to give him the gift. At the gate of the house, he met Sastry's son-in-law and greeted him. Sastry waved to Prabhakar from the door, beckoning him to come in and proudly announced to his son-in-law, "See this. Prabhakar has made a good bargain for such a nice umbrella. I had asked him to buy one for me." He pointed to the umbrella in Prabhakar's hand and took it from him, looking very pleased. The son-in-law glanced at the umbrella and was convinced immediately. "Yes! This is really a good bargain. The quality is very good...and 50 rupees is totally worth it." He looked up at Prabhakar and requested, "Will you buy six such umbrellas for me the next time you go to Bombay, please?" Prabhakar's heart skipped a beat this time. All his math came rushing into his mind and he roughly calculated how much that would cost! The number terrified him, and he was jolted back to the scene. He could manage a fake smile and a nod in the affirmative. He managed a polite response, "Yes...sure." He took leave and, on his way back, he blamed himself for his foolishness. All this, to just keep his impression and ego intact! He reminisces about the incident with much amusement and slight embarrassment, till today.

Over the years of his career at M.E.S., under Sastry's able administration, Prabhakar donned different roles in addition to teaching. He was appointed as Sports Secretary and an NSS[41] Officer during different phases of his tenure. Post his retirement from the college with a remarkable career to look back on, he became the Director of Administration for M.E.S institutions. Prabhakar was also instrumental in building Vidyaranya College and helped with the addition of pre-university and Bachelor of Commerce courses to the Rajajinagar college. The early years of guidance from Professor Sastry was a light that helped Prabhakar walk his path with greater clarity in direction. He flourished as an educator as well as an efficient leader in administration, his mentor being one who had forgotten his own smile, in the process of nurturing innumerable lives.

---

[41] *NSS - National Service Scheme*

Fiat Car

Bangalore, 1985. It was a joyous occasion of a wedding and Rathna and the kids were dressed in grand clothes. Rathna wore the best saree in her wardrobe, a purple Banarasi saree originated from the city of Benares in North India (also known as Varanasi) designed with big flowers threaded in gold. She had lined her eyes with *kajal*, the black eyeliner enhanced the shape of her oval eyes and lastly, she adorned her forehead with a small *bindi* which is an accessory, a tradition in India, mostly among Hindu women. She always preferred to dress simple and did not use any make up, even on special occasions. Yet, she looked radiant and beautiful. Her beauty was always reflected from within, through her warmth and simplicity.

Prabhakar pulled out his red scooter from the garage. The two-seat scooter would conveniently accommodate all five of them on such occasions. Gopi would stand in front where there was space meant to keep small baggage. Mamatha would sit cozily in the middle, between her father and mother and Pannaga would be perched comfortably on Rathna's lap. As they set out to the wedding venue and were halfway there, it began to drizzle. Bangalore rains were known to be unpredictable and no one is ever prepared well in advance for a downpour. Prabhakar rode towards the left and stopped his scooter to find a shelter for them. By then, it was raining heavily and in no time, he, Rathna and the kids were completely drenched. Just as they moved under the shelter of a shop and waited a while, the rain stopped. That is another interesting fact about Bangalore rains. They stop just as quickly as they start! Though the duration of the rain was short and had passed soon, there was no way they could reach the wedding venue in that drenched state. "Let us go back home. We cannot go to the wedding like this," Rathna said, looking at Prabhakar while she was ruffling the hair of the three kids to shake off the rainwater. Prabhakar agreed. They had no choice but to head back home. As they rode back, Prabhakar looked at his family shivering after getting drenched and thought, "I should think of buying a car soon".

A month later, with a loan from his bank, Prabhakar bought a used white 'Fiat car for 30,000 rupees. In those times, owning a car was a big moment in the life of a middle-class family. So, when the car arrived home, there was much joy and excitement. "Car *bantu*[42]! *Hosa*[43] car *bantu*! Our new car has arrived!" squealed the kids. Prabhakar and Rathna were overjoyed with their new purchase. It was another of their

---

[42] *Bantu – arrived in Kannada*
[43] *Hosa – new in Kannada*

dreams to come true. Rathna performed the *puja* and offered prayers for safe and happy travels in the new vehicle. Prabhakar did not know how to drive a car, but he was confident he could learn in a few days. However, when he began his training, it turned out trickier than he imagined. Manual cars needed more effort to maneuver with clutches and gears. Also, the steering was demanding of more muscle power and spontaneity. He found himself getting mixed up with the driving instructions on gear change and other operations. He would often fail to recollect the correct instructions, especially at road intersections and slopes.

"You will have to shift the car from 3rd to 2nd gear by releasing the clutch." "Next, continue to press the brake until you are about to halt." "Now, before your car actually stops, press the clutch and bring the gear in neutral."

By the time he had internalized these instructions and could put them to practice, the car would stop, and as if to rebel, it would start rolling down on slopy roads!

One day, Prabhakar drove the car to a petrol station to fill fuel. He got out of his car, walked a few steps towards the filling station attendant and requested him to fill the tank. The attendant looked behind Prabhakar and then around him. He then looked back at Prabhakar and asked, "Sir...*yelli*? (Where?), Which car sir?" "This one...", Prabhakar answered, turning around with his hand pointed in the direction behind him. He did not see his car! *Where did it vanish? It was here a moment ago!* He looked around frantically and to both his relief and surprise, he saw that the car was at the entrance of the petrol station. He wondered how it got there. He then realized that he had accidentally parked the car in neutral mode and after he got out, it had slowly rolled down and parked itself in front of the air filling pump. He was embarrassed and felt his ears going red. He quickly gathered himself, grinned and said "Oh yes! I forgot to mention...can you please pump air in the tires first and then fill petrol?" The attendant looked at him, surprised and a little confused. He nodded and headed towards the car.

Prabhakar decided to start driving to college, though he was not completely confident in his driving skills yet. He knew that this was the only way he would overcome his fears. One day after college, he was about to head home when his colleague, Mathematics professor Shardamma, waved and called out to him. "Sir. Prabhakar sir! You have come by car, isn't it? Can you please drop me home on your way?" Prabhakar could not refuse, though his mind was not at all sure of offering her the lift. After all, he was not a seasoned driver who could drive more than point to point, and alone at that! He was not used to a co-passenger. He hesitantly opened the door for her and politely ushered her in. The responsibility of driving someone back home safe was literally in his hands now. He started the car and began to drive consciously. As he drove carefully, the clear skies suddenly darkened and it started to rain. This was soon followed by thunder and lightning like heavens were at war. Within a few minutes of the drive, the scene changed. The clouds passed and the sun came up, though the rain had not stopped completely. Prabhakar put on the wipers to clear his view of the front glass pane. The road was getting increasingly harder to see, as the pane was very foggy. To add to this, he had sweat beads forming on his forehead. He only had a memory of the roads that led to her house and that was his only guide now. Shardamma was talking without a break and failed to notice Prabhakar's plight and his nervousness. She was seemingly enjoying the drive and the rain without a care.

Soon, they approached her house. Shardamma waved her hand and gestured to Prabhakar, "Sir *llli nilsi,* (stop here)." He pulled over to the side and stopped. As she got out, she thanked Prabhakar and invited him home. "*Banni⁴⁴, sir. Please come in for a cup of coffee.*" Prabhakar was too preoccupied with his thoughts to enjoy her hospitality then. His only worry was how he would get home! So, he politely refused and nodded. "Not now. Next time, please."

The front windowpane of the car had completely fogged up by then. Prabhakar did not know what to do. He was frustrated. "The wipers are not doing their job!", he thought. He drove a little away from the house after dropping Shardamma and parked again on the side of the road. He lifted his hand to wipe something off the dashboard and accidently touched the window. He was pleasantly surprised that his hand had left a clear line on the window. To his relief, he realized that the window had fogged up from inside! He quickly wiped the window with a handkerchief and smiled to himself. He could see the roads clearly now. It was an exhilarating moment for him. Being a first-time car owner, Prabhakar did not know the technicalities of the vehicle. He had not realized that any warm moisture from inside the car which comes in contact with the cold glass will cause condensation and fog up the windows. If he had switched on the air knob, it would have helped in balancing the temperature of the air inside and outside. This was a discovery for him on the trip that day. As he drove back home, the roads and the rain did not seem bothersome anymore. The drive was easier, too.

Prabhakar continued to learn new mechanisms of the car, but the learning came with a lot of unfavorable incidents. He bumped into sides of auto rickshaws, got shouted at, had vehicles honking at him to move aside every few minutes. He got to hear "*Sariyagi vodsi saar*, (drive carefully, sir)" quite often! He once got so scared of a truck that drove behind him,

---

⁴⁴ *Banni – come in Kannada*

that he turned the steering wheel suddenly to the left and smashed every rear-view mirror of the vehicles parked on the side of the street. His mass destruction caught the attention of onlookers, some of whom owned the vehicles. "*Yenri*[45], what have you done? *Kan kansalva?* ("Can't you see?"), they crowded around him and Prabhakar could only mutter a "sorry...sorry, very sorry", because he realized his blunders and was embarrassed already. As he looked on helplessly at the damage and outrage, he had caused, the traffic police arrived at the scene. He assessed the situation and Prabhakar was sure he would be charged a hefty fine. But as luck would have it, the vehicles were illegally parked and Prabhakar got away without paying any fine for his act.

Prabhakar's family was unaware of his struggles with driving. They were so excited from the time the car was bought that they were waiting to go on a picnic together in the new Fiat. They had chosen their picnic spot too, Lalbagh. Lalbagh is one of Bangalore's famous gardens located in South Bangalore. This botanical garden is an ideal place to spend a few relaxing hours amid refreshing greenery. It was a one-hour drive into the city from their home. Prabhakar agreed but his anxiety grew as he was taking his entire family in the car and to a distant destination through the busy roads of the city. However, he did not express his fear.

On the day of the picnic, Rathna packed lunch and the picnic baskets. The kids were jumping in excitement. "Picnic, picnic! Lalbagh, Lalbagh!", they screamed in chorus. Prabhakar put the picnic baskets into the car and they set out. After about 10 minutes of driving, Prabhakar turned to a small intersection and parked the car. As Rathna looked out, trying to see where and why he had stopped the car, he declared, "This is where the

---

[45] *Yenri – What in Kannada*

picnic will be! Come, come, let us go to the park." Rathna was surprised. The kids were confused too. They looked around and noticed a small park in the middle of the busy intersection. There was a bench and a small patch of grass in the "park". "This is not Lalbagh!", Rathna thought. But, by then she had gauged her husband's agony. He was nervous to drive that far to Lalbagh. She started giggling and when the kids understood the situation, they joined in as well. It was a hilarious scene, a family of five laughing loudly on the side of a busy road, as buses and vehicles passed by. Rathna reached for the picnic basket and they had their 'picnic' lunch at the dusty intersection. It was not exactly a day out in Lalbagh as they had planned, but memories of this day were something they cherished with joy for years to come.

After this episode of the failed picnic, Prabhakar realized that no matter how much he tried, driving a car was not his cup of tea. He decided to give away the Fiat to his brother-in-law in Mysore. Years later, he bought another car and employed a driver. Prabhakar accepted his shortcoming and for once, his confidence and optimism did not win. He accepted that not everything is meant for everyone and learned that certain shortcomings are to be faced and let go. He had not totally lost, though. He had gained many interesting stories of his experience with driving the car that he could later share with his family.

Marriage Tales
and Life Now

Karnataka meets Kerala

"A boy from another caste? I never expected this...", Rathna teared up as she said these words, probably for the tenth time or more, after Mamatha had made the announcement.

When Mamatha, their first daughter, announced to Prabhakar and Rathna that she had chosen Sumit, her school and college mate as her life partner, Rathna was shaken. "I had always envisioned our oldest daughter...our first born, to be married to a boy that we would choose and arrange an alliance with. But now..." The sudden decision from her daughter was a blow that had killed her dream.

Mamatha was well-educated and there were so many alliances of the same caste that were coming her way. Rathna had been keenly looking at which of them would best suit her dear daughter and this news shattered her beyond words. Prabhakar, however, handled the news a little better. He, as a college professor, had seen the changing times. Young adults were choosing their own life partners and he knew Sumit well. Sumit had been his student and he belonged to a good family. But Sumit being from a different caste and culture - "Would he assimilate into our family of orthodox cultures and traditions? Would it not be a challenge?", Prabhakar thought but pushed these concerns aside. He would worry about all such issues later. For now, his concern was different and more important. Sumit did not have a job yet and he needed to talk to him about it. He called Sumit over and sat down to talk. "I understand that you both love each other and want to get married. I will give you three years' time. In that duration, if you can settle down with a job and you both still want to get married, we will conduct the wedding. However, if either of you has had a change of heart during the time, I will respect that as well". Sumit was pleasantly surprised at how well Prabhakar had handled the situation and given him a generous offer of time. He had seen his friends who were in the same boat as him. They were in love, but the parents were either opposing their decisions or forcefully marrying their daughters off to someone of their choice. He agreed and thanked Prabhakar for all the understanding and right guidance.

Meanwhile, in those three years, Prabhakar had a task at hand, too. How would he manage this inter-caste alliance? Nobody in his family had married outside the caste. The history of caste system in India is a very complicated and highly controversial topic. Its evolution is said to date back to 1500 BC, when Hindu civilization transformed into a hierarchical society and gave designations based on occupation to four primary subunits. 'Brahmanas' were priests and teachers, 'Kshtriyas' were warriors and rulers, 'Vaishyas' were farmers and traders and 'Shudras' and 'Dalits' were laborers. New doctrines and rigid superstitions over centuries forced a social institution that created these groups of castes. Marriages were strictly within the same caste so that the economical background, customs, and traditions were broadly matched. Although now, urban areas have different attitudes towards inter-caste marriages, some orthodox families still associate the word 'disgrace' to inter-caste marriages. Statistics show that only 5% of Indian marriages are inter-caste marriages, even today. So back then, as Prabhakar convinced his relatives of the alliance, he encouraged them to see the changing rigidities of the caste system. He boldly announced his decision to support this alliance, stating that he was ready to be the change. With Prabhakar's consent given, the relatives eventually stopped bringing same caste alliances for Mamatha. Rathna too wholeheartedly accepted Sumit as her future son-in-law.

In due course, Sumit got a good job and came back to Prabhakar, asking for Mamatha's hand in marriage. After the date was fixed, Prabhakar started planning for the wedding. Sumit's family belonged to the South Indian state of Kerala and their native language was Malayalam. There is a vast cultural difference between Karnataka and Kerala and the way weddings are conducted in the two states. Prabhakar asked Sumit to lend him a few Malayali wedding videos to understand their rituals.

Rathna sat along with Prabhakar to watch the videos, but she was utterly disappointed. She was expecting an elaborate wedding ritual, like the weddings in Karnataka. The Kerala style weddings were very different though and among the simplest ones she had ever seen! The bride and groom exchange garlands and wedding rings and as a last step, the groom ties the *mangalsutra,* which is a necklace that the groom ties around the neck of the bride, which would then on announce her identity as a married woman.

All the rituals were completed in no time! Rathna started to cry, "What? What is this? Where is the *VaraPuje*[46], *Gowripuje*[47], *Kanyadhana*[48]? Not even *Saptapadi*[49]? What kind of marriage is this?!" She was aghast to see only a 3-step wedding which took just a little more than three minutes in all, as against the 3-day wedding traditions in Karnataka!

In Karnataka, the wedding rituals begin with a ceremony called *Vara Puje,* where the bridegroom is welcomed by the bride's family and a few rituals are conducted specifically for the *groom.* The second day is marked for *Gowri Puje* where the bride seeks goddess Gowri's blessings. The Goddess's own marriage is a symbol of everlasting love and the bride seeks blessings for her marriage to be the same. This is followed by *Kanyadhana*, a ritual in which the parents do the *dhana* - offer of their *kanya* - daughter, to the groom, as his equal partner. Hindu tradition believes that one's daughter is the biggest asset that one can give away in life and Rathna was looking forward to having this privilege. She did not want her daughter and her groom to miss their most important ritual either - the

---

[46] *Varapuje – a ritual to welcome the bridegroom*
[47] *Gowripuje – Prayers to Goddess Gowri.*
[48] *Kanyadhana – a ritual of giving the bride to join her groom*
[49] *Saptapadi – a ritual of seven vows in Hindu tradition.*

Saptapadi - where the groom and the bride take seven steps around *Agni*, the holy fire amidst the seven vows of marriage chanted by the priest. Prabhakar heard all Rathna's wishes and only nodded. His mind raced as he wondered, "How will I get all these dreams fulfilled?"

Prabhakar met Sumit's mother and explained his predicament to her. He proposed an idea of a fusion wedding and she agreed. The most modernized wedding stage was set up. All the rituals from Karnataka were duly completed, followed by the short wedding rituals from Kerala. People who witnessed the ceremony said that it had set a precedent and was the most beautiful fusion wedding they had attended thus far.

After all the ceremonies concluded, the couple sought blessings from all the elders who had gathered. Prabhakar looked at his daughter and son-in-law and was overcome with emotion. His mind went back to a moment from the wedding. One of the rituals of Karnataka is welcoming the groom by the bride's parents. The ritual involved washing of the groom's feet which is done by the father of the bride. This ritual originated from the belief that the groom is Lord Shiva himself. The tradition of washing his feet meant holding the highest respect for the groom. Sumit, however, had politely but firmly refused this ritual. "I am sorry, but I cannot let my teacher wash my feet. I respect him and this would mean allowing an act of disrespect," he had said, folding his hands. Prabhakar and all the guests present at the wedding were dazed by this noble thought.

His son-in-law's deep-rooted values assured Prabhakar that he was indeed the right partner for his daughter. He felt a sense of relief and satisfaction, too. He was able to conduct the celebration successfully and everyone was happy. But he also felt an inexplicable sadness. His little princess who grew up to be this beautiful woman belonged to another family now and would go far away from him. Prabhakar knew that every girl's father experienced this bitter-sweet moment at some point in life. He felt as if his mind was still not ready to send her away, but will a father ever be ready?

Runaway Bride

Gopi was of marriageable age and had started getting good alliances through the family circle. One such was through Rajeshwari. She suggested an alliance for him from a family living in Mysore, a widowed mother with her three daughters. The alliance was sought for the eldest of the daughters. "The family is not very financially well off, but a respectable one. The girl is educated and eligible for marriage. I feel she will be a good match for our Gopi, "Rajeshwari had strongly recommended. Prabhakar and Rathna too were keen on pursuing talks with the family. After all the formal discussions between the elders and with the agreement of the girl and Gopi, the date of the wedding was fixed.

Prabhakar was excited to make the arrangements. He wanted nothing but the best wedding for his soft-spoken and only son. Most of the relatives being in Mysore, it was more convenient to conduct the wedding there. He booked a hall in Mysore and made the other bookings as well - decorations, catering, etc. The invitations were sent, and purchases were almost done. As the date neared, the ambience was joyful and everyone in the family was busy. Prabhakar and Rathna looked forward to the big day. They were excited about bringing home a new member to the family - a wife to Gopi; a daughter to them.

It was only a week until the wedding. Prabhakar was looking into his checklist and ticking off tasks and writing down a few new ones. Just then he received a phone call. It was from the bride's grandfather who began the conversation addressing with respect "Prabhakar avare[50], how do I convey this to you...? My granddaughter. The bride-to-be has disappeared with a boy from our street. She was apparently in love with him...none of us knew about it..." Prabhakar's heart skipped a beat. He sat down heavily on the chair and continued to listen. He stared into space and his mind went blank. He could not believe what he had just heard. His first thought was, "*Nobody had forced the wedding on her. Then, why had she not revealed her intentions to anyone?*". Her grandfather was crying at the other end of the line. In between sobs, he apologized, "We are very sorry. Really sorry. It is a matter of such shame...I do not know what more to say. She has left us a letter...saying that she was in love with someone else. And she was going along with plans only so that she could...she could buy time to execute her plan." He continued to cry. Prabhakar was enraged to hear this. The wedding was only a week away! He had paid for everything: the marriage hall, invitations, gold ornaments, sarees, etc. They had also handed over the ornaments and wedding sarees to the girl. How could she do this? Apart from the financial loss,

---

[50] *Avare – sign of respect in Kannada, equivalent to sir/madam.*

Prabhakar just could not understand why anyone would do such a thing without a second thought! He did not know how to respond. The conversation ended abruptly, and he mindlessly placed the phone receiver back on the hook.

With a heavy heart, Prabhakar shared the news with his family and everyone was shocked and pained. They were at a total loss. Rathna and Prabhakar were hurt beyond words and could not comprehend the situation. Their older daughter Mamatha too had married someone she had loved and chosen, but she had approached her parents with the truth, seeking their consent. Prabhakar had appreciated that and assumed that the younger generation had the maturity to be frank and open about their choices. What went wrong here? Was the family not open enough for the girl to communicate her feelings to them?

Prabhakar rushed to Mysore to the girl's house. He found the mother grieving and embarrassed to see him. She could hardly bring herself to speak to Prabhakar and was continuously crying. Prabhakar was distressed to see their helplessness and decided to see what he could do. He started his own enquiries and after a couple of days, he traced the couple's whereabouts. They had travelled to the village of Subramanya and gotten married in a temple. The couple was found and escorted back to Mysore.

The family was angry, and hell broke loose after the couple was brought to the girl's house. Prabhakar intervened and asked the mother and grandfather to calm down. "Forget what happened. You cannot change the past. Now think of what is to be done", he urged them. "I would like you to conduct their wedding in the same hall that I had booked for Gopi", he added. The girl's family was deeply touched and obliged to Prabhakar for making this offer. They could not thank him enough.

Meanwhile in Bangalore, everyone was still fretting about the unfortunate incident. When Prabhakar returned home and narrated the events of the past couple of days in Mysore, Rathna was moved and could not stop her tears. Everyone praised Prabhakar for what he had done to help the runaway bride and her family. Anyone else in his position would have created a ruckus and demanded financial recovery. Prabhakar had not only accepted the reality of the situation, but also handled the entire situation with dignity and poise.

Days passed. Rathna was still worried about Gopi and was constantly lost in thought. She wondered why they had to face such a situation. Prabhakar consoled her saying, "I am sure there is something good in this. We are destined to get someone else. One who would fit with our family better. Let us wait. " He also sensed what Gopi must be going through. Prabhakar pacified him as well. "Gopi, you know...I am actually relieved that this incident occurred now and not later. Now there is still no emotional investment in this relationship. If this had happened after the wedding and the girl was not happy with the situation, it would have been a disaster...for you, her, and all of us". Gopi was mature enough to understand. He agreed with his father and was happy to move on.

In a year, Gopi found his beautiful bride in Chaithra. She was a charming, simple, and mature girl, a real perfect match for Gopi. The family rejoiced and the wedding was conducted with fun and festivities. All was well, as it ended well.

Prabhakar uses this incident as an example when speaking to youngsters. He encourages them to talk to their parents without fear. He strongly believes that lying only brings pain and shame to all and results in undesirable complications. He feels that this can be avoided if every situation in the family can be worked out peacefully with the involvement of loved ones. His lifelong advice to one and all could be summarized thus: "There is always going to be calm after a storm. But you need to first face and withstand the fury of the storm. If your loved ones are venting, have the courage to stand by them and explain where you come from as well. With all sides heard and understood, there will certainly be an amicable solution."

Separation and a wedding

"I am so proud of you, Panna! You have realized your dream of pursuing your higher studies abroad!" Prabhakar was exhilarated when his third child, Pannaga gave the news of her admission to a master's program in San Diego, USA. Prabhakar always advocated for higher studies and believed in equipping every child with the best education he/she can possibly get. So, this news was indeed a very special and celebratory one for him. Rathna was very happy, too, but as a mother, she was a bit worried. She would have preferred to see her daughter married and settled first. But she also knew that Panna, as Pannaga was fondly called, was the most capable and mature of the three children and would manage on her own very well. So, with whole-hearted acceptance and all their wishes and blessings, their lucky 'eclipse' daughter Panna set off to the US to fulfill her dream.

After Panna finished her studies, Prabhakar and Rathna arranged her marriage with a suitable boy. She was married off with all the rituals and traditions that Rathna had always wished for. However, fate showed its dark side once again to the family. Two years into her marriage, Panna expressed to her parents that the relationship had not been compatible and explained her woes to them. "I tried my best to make this marriage work", she poured out all her feelings in between sobs. "Tell me...what should I do now? I have been through a lot of pain and struggle to make it work." Prabhakar and Rathna listened patiently and consoled her. It was yet another blow and another challenge that life had thrown at them. They contemplated the situation. Separation and divorce were not common in their times and generation. As they sat together quietly watching the sunset through the window of their home, pondering about the worries of their daughter, Rathna spoke with moist eyes. "In our times, there were heavy compromises made either by the husband or wife and the relationship somehow continued. Most of the marriages were just maintained for the sake of society, parents or children." Rathna had been a witness to many such relationships in her life and had seen the emotional turmoil one had to bear through the process. She had seen people becoming lonely and tired. She would always look at them and wonder if what they did was worthwhile. Now with their own daughter in such a situation, she questioned herself. "How can I tell her to maintain the relationship and see her unhappy throughout her life?", she thought.

Prabhakar too had a similar outlook. He had given enough relationship advice to many, only to realize that if two people were not happy, then living a lie together just to please the family and society was meaningless. He was convinced and decided, *"I do not want my daughter to carry the burden of an unhappy relationship all her life. Life is too short and sweet."*

Prabhakar and Rathna did not have the support of their parents to lean on in difficult times, but they had made up their mind that they would always be there for their children. Now, again, they knew what they had to do to keep the promise they had made to themselves. Prabhakar called Panna and assured her of their complete support and an amicable separation. A few people voiced concerns about Panna's future but Prabhakar stood behind her like a rock handling the situation, not letting a single voice blame her. The separation was smooth and completed legally within a few months.

Panna moved on with her life and met Varun a couple of years later. She told her parents about her desire to marry him. Prabhakar knew in his heart that fate had played a role in bringing the best for his daughter. Prabhakar and Rathna blessed Panna and Varun and their wedding was celebrated soon after. Again, all was well that ended well.

Prabhakar often looked back at the lives of his three children and the unique stories around their marriages. He had handled each of them with dignity and grace. With every incident, there was a take-away which he shared as advice to others. With Panna's marriage story, his advice to parents was to listen to their children. "They have only you to understand them unconditionally. If they are not happy with their lives, do not ask them to remain in it forever, for any reason. They must have, most probably, tried everything they could and approached you only as a last resort for help."

He always reiterated the importance of parental support in every situation and assured that smiles arising from the true happiness of children is priceless.

Glimpses Past and Present

At a reunion in Mysore with his old friends from school, Prabhakar was sharing nostalgic moments from his life. His friends too had many stories to tell and each of them narrated theirs. Together, they relived the memories of good old school days, their carefree years, their teachers, and the pranks they played. Prabhakar was joking that until recently he would get nightmares of how he would complete his studies or how he would feed his family, only to wake up sweating and be relieved to realize that he was already retired!

Prabhakar had channeled this irremediable restlessness into strength and energy to help uplift others. Throughout his life, Prabhakar had been involved in several community and social services. He continued to do so even after retirement. While he was a chairperson for NSS camps, he had organized trips to open jails where youngsters could personally meet and interview criminals. Their stories were intriguing and an eye-opener to them. The inmates had explained how they regretted their actions and that by the time they realized their grave mistakes, it had been too late. They confessed that they had acted on impulse and committed horrendous crimes. Prabhakar had been successful in inspiring the youngsters through a real-life campaign. He strongly believed that this first-hand experience would have an impact in the long run to keep youngsters from reacting impulsively and resorting to violence.

Prabhakar had also worked in villages for long periods of time, sometimes months together during summers. His aim was to build better roads in these villages to ease the lives of the village folk. He had formed a team of young volunteers for this project and completed it successfully. He also led an initiative of planting trees and motivated volunteers to plant as many as 1000 trees. He took up many other such impactful projects and led them to completion.

Prabhakar always believed in positive results of good deeds, however small or big they may be. He advocated the same to his students and assured them that the impact of a good deed would always be multifold. A recent incident touched Prabhakar deeply. A vegetable vendor came to meet him, along with his daughter. "Sir, this is for the Student Welfare Fund of the college," he said, humbly handing out a cheque of 10,000 rupees. Prabhakar was astonished. He looked at the man and the bright-eyed girl, who was gleaming with pride. He wondered who they were and why they had made this generous donation. The vendor smiled at Prabhakar, placed his hand on the girl's shoulder and said "Sir, you may not remember us. But you are the reason my daughter is standing here now, as an achiever." "Oh yes, yes! Now I do remember you...,"Prabhakar smiled at the two of them and recalled how the girl had scored a high percentage in school, but the father did not have enough money to support his daughter's college education. Prabhakar had arranged for a sponsor just in time for her admission. A rich businessman had come to enroll his daughter too at college around the same time. Prabhakar had spoken to him about the vegetable vendor's brilliant daughter and urged him to take on the expense of her education. The rest was history. "Sir..." Prabhakar was jolted back to the present by the voice. "Sir, I want to pay it forward and help another needy child," the man said and took leave. Prabhakar was filled with mixed emotions as he watched the father-daughter make their way home. This vegetable vendor who still pushed carts to sell vegetables had become the proud father of a daughter, who secured a rank in the state exams. One good deed had made a huge impact and now, led to another.

Once he was well-settled and financially stable, Prabhakar himself sponsored many deserving students for their higher education. He dreamed of a world where no child would lose the opportunity to be educated, just because of lack of finances. He hoped that each of the children he helped would someday pay this forward. This chain would help realize his dream to a large extent.

Prabhakar had started the Teachers' Welfare Fund in M.E.S. College. The staff and management were highly appreciative of his initiative and offered full support. It was a simple scheme where all teachers contributed a small amount towards the welfare fund. They could take personal loans from the collected funds and when a teacher retired, they got a share of the amount for the number of years of their service. Since pension funds took time to process and be available, this fund at the time of retirement helped teachers attend to their immediate expenses. Prabhakar's foresight had earned him many thankful hearts.

Prabhakar often reflects on his life and the stories of his past revisit him occasionally at different junctures of his life. He gratefully recollects incidents when he was able to help people in need, both monetarily and otherwise.

Once his friend had approached Prabhakar for monetary help for his mother's treatment and eventually to cover costs for her last rites. Prabhakar stepped in to help by taking a loan to cover the expenses. His heartfelt prayer to God has always been to fill his pockets so that he can give to others generously.

Another story that is etched in his memory is of a young driver Srinivasa, who had come to Bangalore in search of a job. He got employed in Prabhakar's household as their family driver. Srinivasa, who was around 18 years of age at the time, was a bold and smart worker. Prabhakar had taken an immediate liking to him. Srinivasa would drive the family to different venues, family functions and places of worship. In India, there was and still is a perception that manual work is a low stature job. People belonging to the class of drivers, truck drivers, peons, house help, waiters and so on, are treated with some amount of indignity and not given due respect. The social conduct rules in India are apparent and there is a strong credence that the social status of people doing such jobs is somehow of less standing than a person working in an office space. This attitude brings out undesirable behaviors towards them from people who consider themselves from a higher stratum of society. They welcome family and friends with a cup of coffee or snacks but offer the same in separate cups and plates to a household help or driver. This callous, insensitive attitude is still seen in many households. In contrast,

Prabhakar and Rathna treated Srinivasa like a member of their family. When Srinivasa once got infected with tuberculosis and was hospitalized, he was scared as he was new to the city and all alone in his illness. Prabhakar took care of him and nurtured him back to good health. With Prabhakar's help and guidance, Srinivasa owns a transportation company today and is doing well.

Prabhakar himself did many odd jobs during his lifetime to feed his family. He strongly advocates dignity of labor and says there is nothing to be ashamed of with any job that one undertakes to earn a living. His message: Whatever the job, do it with all honesty and sincerity.

Through the many years of struggle in their life, Prabhakar and Rathna were bound together, supporting each other unconditionally. Life had thrown many challenges at them, none of them easy. When Rathna was battling her kidney failure, Prabhakar was distraught. It was certainly not something he had prepared for or knew how to deal with. She had been his pillar of strength all through and to see her weaken physically and mentally was very painful for him.

Many times, he saw Rathna lose hope, but her faith in her gods was unshakable. It kept her strong and lifted her spirits up whenever she was on the edge. Even through her suffering, she would pray for a dignified death. Prabhakar was not the one to accept defeat and let her go. He would get her the required medical attention in time, even for the slightest of symptoms. He always kept an eye out for any change in her health pattern. For years, Prabhakar remained her primary caregiver, and with the support of his children, he devoted all his time for her care and comfort. But fate had its way, as always.

When Rathna lost her battle to death, she left Prabhakar with words that he would always treasure. She said that she wanted him to be her husband for all seven lives to come. It is a popular Hindu belief that when a marriage is solemnized, the two souls are destined to be together for seven lifetimes. Prabhakar wondered how, despite all his imperfections and the struggles he had put his wife through, could she wish for this! She had answered him with the familiar smile that had lit up his good and bad days for years now. She followed it up with a few words that Prabhakar treasures most - "A diamond with a little rough edge is still a diamond and will remain one always." To him, she was more precious than a diamond; his own gem, his Rathna.

Not a day passes without Prabhakar expressing gratitude for his life and the amazing journey he has been on. With all its lessons and hardships, life also ultimately brought him the best moments and due success in all aspects. He has no complaints or regrets and believes that there is a reason for everything that happens in one's life. "Life is a continuum of journeys, crossroads and a series of stories..." Prabhakar continues his journey of learning, doing and wholeheartedly experiencing every moment, every single day.

Now at the age of 75, Prabhakar still looks forward to helping as many people as he can and contributing towards social initiatives. He now lives a contented life with his son and family in his house 'Jayasheela' in Bangalore. He occasionally visits his daughters in the United States of America. His family now includes six grandchildren, sons-in-law, and daughter-in-law.

Bare, yet giving.
Nurtured, loved, lost
Yet, giving.
Of its barest branches,
Some love to hold on.
The wings to rest,
Before the flight again

K.G. Prabhakar

The Team

Pannaga

Suma

Karthik

Raji

Mamatha

Raghu

Sidhant

Sumit

Samarth

Made in the USA
Las Vegas, NV
24 October 2020